WEST END SYRACUSE LIBRARY
Y0-ATB-725

JEWISH HOLIDAY PARTY BOOK

A Practical Guide to Parties
Planned for Children Ages 5 to 12

By

LILLIAN S. ABRAMSON
and
LILLIAN T. LEIDERMAN

New York
BLOCH PUBLISHING COMPANY

6449

Copyright, 1966, by

BLOCH PUBLISHING COMPANY, INC.

Second Revised Edition, 1966.

LIBRARY OF CONGRESS CATALOG NUMBER 54-11436

PRINTED IN THE UNITED STATES OF AMERICA

INTRODUCTION

Some of the warmest memories we cherish are those of childhood when we gathered with friends and family in the celebration of some special event. How much greater is that impression if, as children, we were given the opportunity to participate in the planning, the preparation and the execution of the celebration.

As we look over the Jewish calendar we find specific times of the year set aside for certain holidays. What meanings will these occasions have for the child of today? Will they be just holidays they have learned about but soon to be forgotten? Or will they become an integral part of the child's life?

Most of the Jewish holidays lend themselves naturally to parties for children: Chanukah is the time for giving gifts, playing games, lighting candles; Purim is the time for pageantry and masquerade; Lag B'Ómer is the time for outings and picnics; etc.

While suggestions made have proven themselves with many children, each party-giver knows her own group of guests and the circumstances under which she must work. The parties, as planned by the authors, can be simplified or elaborated upon, depending upon the needs of the children involved.

This book, written as a practical guide for the mother in the home, is also intended for use by the teacher in the school.

We have tried to make some of the directions simple enough so that even the children themselves can follow.

We sincerely hope this little volume will provide you with ideas for many happy Holiday Parties.

L.S.A.

L.T.L.

WHEN WILL YOUR PARTY BE?

Jewish Holidays do not fall on specific dates of the general calendar. The dates vary from year to year since they are based on the Jewish or lunar calendar. It is possible, however, to predict the approximate period of occurrence. This list should be helpful. It contains the party occasions mentioned in this book and their probable dates.

1) Rosh Hashanah ....Sometime in September
2) Succoth ....Beginning of October
3) Simchat Torah ....Sometime in October
4) Chanukah ....Sometime in December
5) Tu B'Shvat ....Sometime in January
6) Purim ....Sometime in March
7) Passover ....Sometime in April
8) Israel Independence Day.Beginning of May
9) Lag B'Omer ....Sometime in May
10) Shavuoth ....Sometime in June
11) Sabbath ....Every Saturday
12) New Month ....Beginning of each Hebrew month

PARTY HINTS

1) The number of children invited should depend upon the facilities, the adult supervision and the age range of the guests. Generally—the younger the age level, the fewer the guests.

2) Encourage the child-host to participate in the planning and actual preparation, even if he can only lick the stamps on the invitations or fold the napkins.

3) Invitations should be mailed out about one week or ten days before the party.

4) You can have a great deal of fun making decorations for room and table. There are, however, many commercial products which can be purchased, such as napkins, tablecloths and hats, with holiday motifs.

5) Diagrams for invitations, place cards, etc. should be followed in the exact dimensions presented, except where noted.

6) The difficult time of a party is when the guests are arriving. Children may get into lots of mischief waiting around for a party to begin. This is a good time to make use of the recommended holiday records. If possible, have a spot set up with reading, coloring books, etc. for the guests to use while waiting.

7) Don't have the party lag. As soon as a game ceases to be of interest switch to another game or to the next part of the program.

8) A good party usually lasts between one and a half hours to three hours. As a general rule, the younger the children, the shorter the party.
HAVE FUN!

CONTENTS

ROSH HASHANAH
HAPPY NEW YEAR PARTY

THE OCCASION

Rosh Hashanah is the beginning of the Jewish Year. It is the time when parents and children go to the synagogue to recall their deeds of the past year and to pray that the year ahead should be a good one and a sweet one. At the Synagogue special prayers are said and the Shofar is blown. At home, special foods are placed on the dinner table. These foods are round challahs, apples and honey.

September is the beginning of many new things for children. It is a nice time for them to have a party since it gives them the opportunity of inviting friends whom they might not have seen all summer long.

WE INVITE THE GUESTS

The invitation is in the form of an apple. Trace Figure 1 on to red construction paper. Cut out two copies of Figure 1 and put them together by Scotch taping along the outer edges. Cut apple through on dotted line so that the top of the apple is completely separated from the bottom. Cut out a slightly smaller apple of white paper (omit the stem). Insert it into the top portion of the red apple and write the message on front and back (Figure 2). Slip Figure 2 into the bottom portion of the apple.

Figure 1

Tape

The summer is gone.
Rosh Hashanah is here.
Let us get together
To greet the New Year.

Jonathan

Figure 2

Date_____
Time_____
Place_____
_____

Back of
Figure 2

WE DECORATE THE ROOM AND TABLE

All New Years cards received by the family could be placed attractively around the room. Some suggestions: stand cards up on mantlepiece above a fireplace; before holiday starts, string narrow ribbon or cord across the ceiling and hang cards; attach cards to wall to form a Jewish star.

A place card at each setting is in the form of a shofar. Fold a 4"x4" piece of construction paper in half. Trace Figure 4 on to construction paper by placing points A and B on the fold. Except for the three notches, points A and B should not be cut through.

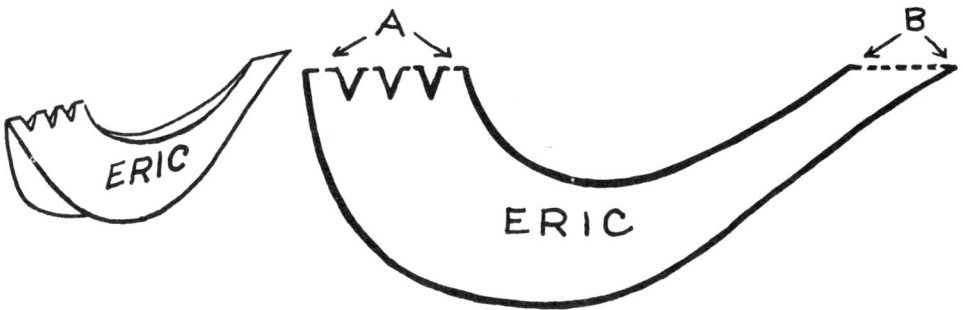

The centerpiece on the table is a large round chalah. The numbers of the New Year are cut out of yellow oak tag to form a ring around the challah, or make a crown out of oak tag. On this write the number of the New Year and decorate with glitter. Place crown around the chalah.

11

TIME TO EAT

SUGGESTED MENU:

Little round chalah at each setting
Apple and honey plate
Apple juice
Basket with raisins, nuts and candy

Apple and honey plate—cut apple into wedges with an apple cutter. Arrange wedges around the outer edges of the plate. Place a little paper cup filled with honey in the center of the plate.

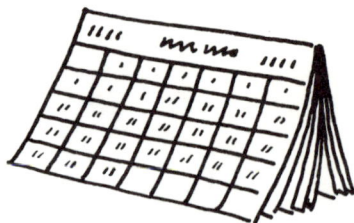

A FAVOR FOR EACH CHILD

A calendar for the New Year. These can be obtained from neighborhood banks or stores.

12

GAMES ARE FUN

1) Treasure Hunt:
    Write the name of each of the twelve Hebrew months on separate sheets of paper. Hide the sheets in the room or within the party area. The child who finds the most months wins.

Tishri	Sh'vat	Sivan
Cheshvan	Adar	Tamuz
Kislev	Nisan	Av
Tevet	Iyar	Elul

2) The Most Holidays?
    Who can name the most Jewish holidays in the year? Give a time limit of about one minute.

3) Guess the Holiday:
    A child thinks of a Jewish holiday and gives one hint. The one who guesses correctly has the next turn to be 'up.' Here are some sample hints:

    This holiday comes every week. (Shabbat)
    We use loud noisemakers. (Purim)
    We march around the Synagogue. (Simchat Torah)
    We light special candles. (Chanukah)

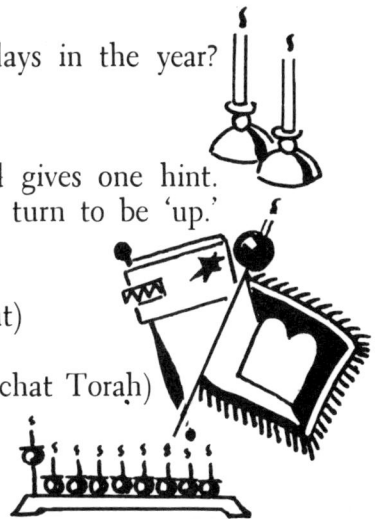

4) L'Shanah Tovah:
    One child is 'it' and closes his eyes. The leader points to another child who calls out the New Year greeting, "L'Shanah Tovah." 'It' opens his eyes and tries to guess whose voice he heard.

5) Memory of Objects:
    Place some Rosh Hashanah objects in a central place, e.g. apple, honey, Shofar, challah, Torah, Jewish star, etc. Children study objects. One child closes his eyes while another removes one object. The first child opens his eyes and guesses which object was removed. (Pictures may be used.)

13

6) Calendar Game:
    Use a large calendar. Who can find a Jewish holiday first? Who can find his birthday? Can he give the Hebrew date?

7) Make a Wish:
    Children take turns making a wish for the New Year.

THE PARTY FROM BEGINNING TO END

1) Game: L'Shanah Tovah Greetings
2) Treasure Hunt
3) Game: Memory of Objects
4) Eat
5) Make a Wish (at the table)
6) Calendar Game
7) Guess the Holiday or the most Holidays
8) Home

MATERIALS NEEDED FOR THE PARTY

For the Invitations: red construction paper, white paper, Scotch tape.

For the Place Cards: colored construction paper.

For the Centerpiece: round challah (large), yellow oak tag, glitter.

For the Room: New Year cards received by the family, narrow ribbon or string, Scotch tape.

For the Games: twelve small sheets of paper for the Treasure Hunt, a large calendar, objects for the Memory Game.

For the Souvenirs: a small Hebrew calendar for each guest.

SUCCOTH PARTY

THE OCCASION

Succoth, a fall festival, comes at harvest time when the fruits and vegetables are gathered. It is also the holiday when we recall that the Hebrews dwelt in huts (or Succahs) on their journey from Egypt through the desert to the land of Israel. During the Succoth Week meals are traditionally served in the Succah.

Children can have a gay time with a party of their own. Any day during the week of Succoth is a good time to have this party.

WE INVITE THE GUESTS

The invitation is in the form of a Succah. By opening the door, the guest will see the message which is inside.

Trace the outline of Figure 1 on to colored construction paper and cut out 2 copies of contrasting colors for each invitation. Decorate one copy and cut the door on dotted line, as show in Figure 1. On the other copy, write the message as shown in Figure 2.

15

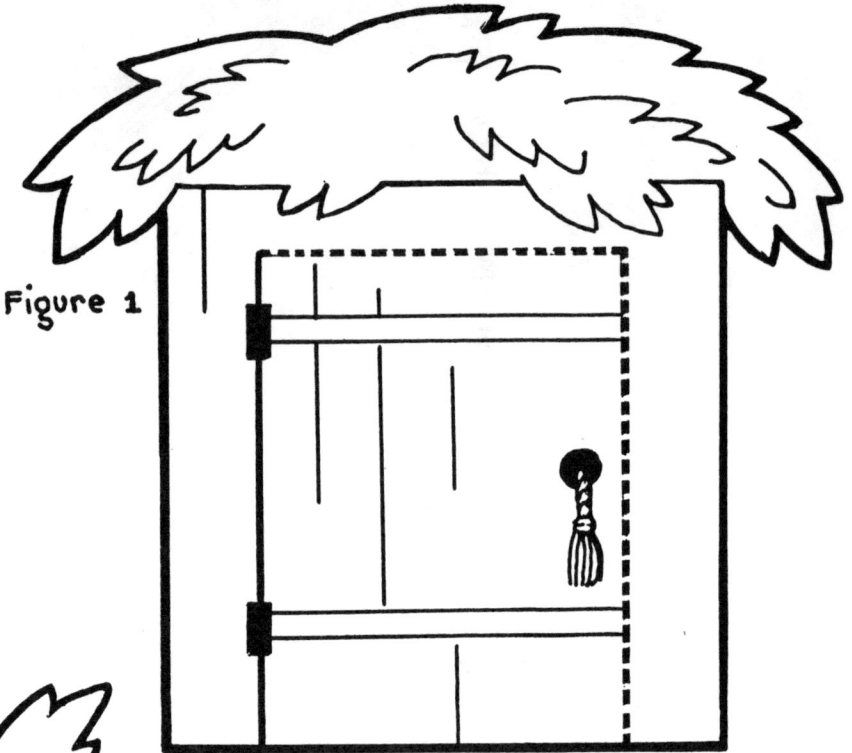

Figure 1

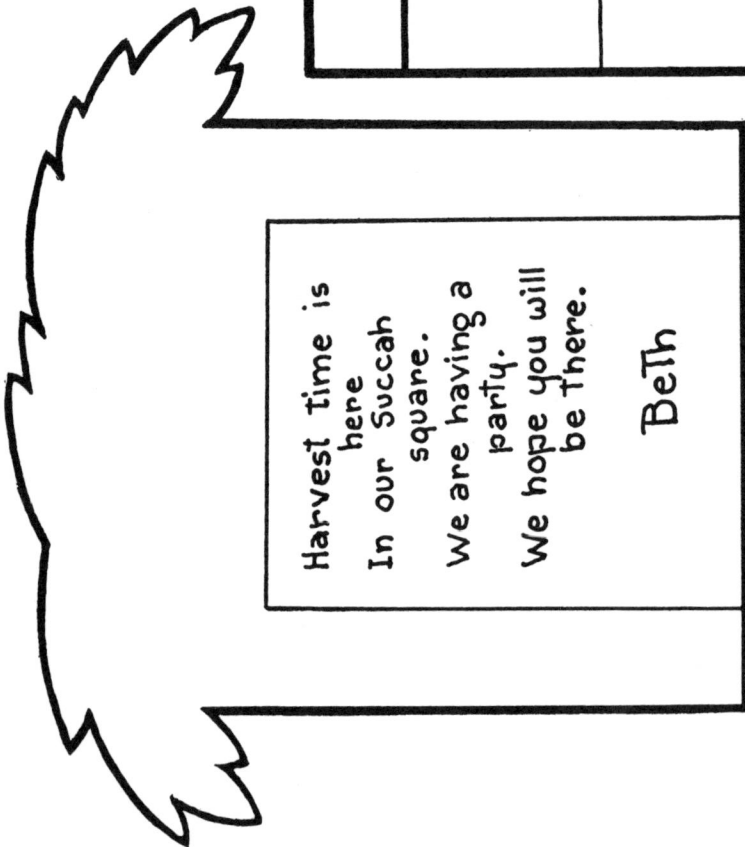

Harvest time is
here
In our Succah
square.
We are having a
party.
We hope you will
be there.

BeTh

Figure 2

Paste Figure 1 on Figure 2, leaving the door free to swing open. The specific information as to day, time and place may be written either on back of door or back of invitation.

WE DECORATE THE ROOM

If possible, have this party in a real Succah, either your own or in a community Succah. If a Succah is not available, decorate your own dining room to resemble one. String green crepe paper or twine across the ceiling. Attach leaves or branches and fruit.

Be sure to have a Lulav and Ethrog prominently on display.

WE DECORATE THE TABLE

A large pumpkin, scooped and dried, will make a lovely centerpiece. Fill this with wrapped favors to which are attached colored streamers which end at each setting.

The place cards can be decorated with an Ethrog. To make this, trace Figure 3 on to pastel-colored construction paper, cut on dotted line and fold the two side pieces back so that the card can stand.

Now, take a piece of plain white paper and, with a soft black pencil, trace the outline of an Ethrog as shown in Figure 4. Cut out around the heavy black line.

Place the cut-out Ethrog in the center of the card. With your thumb, rub the black line in an outward motion so that the black smudge comes on the card. When the cut-out is removed, there is a clear shape of an Ethrog in which space you may write the guest's name.

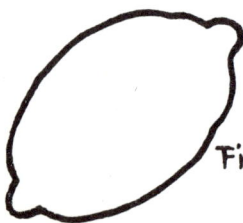

Figure 4

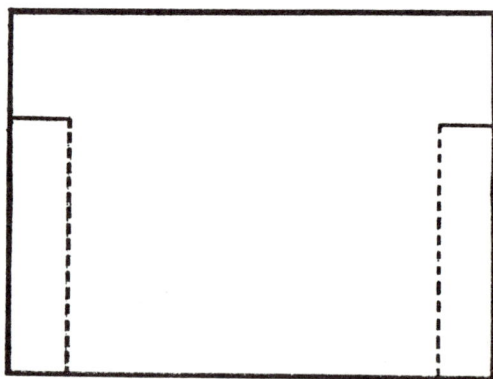

Figure 3

Figure 5

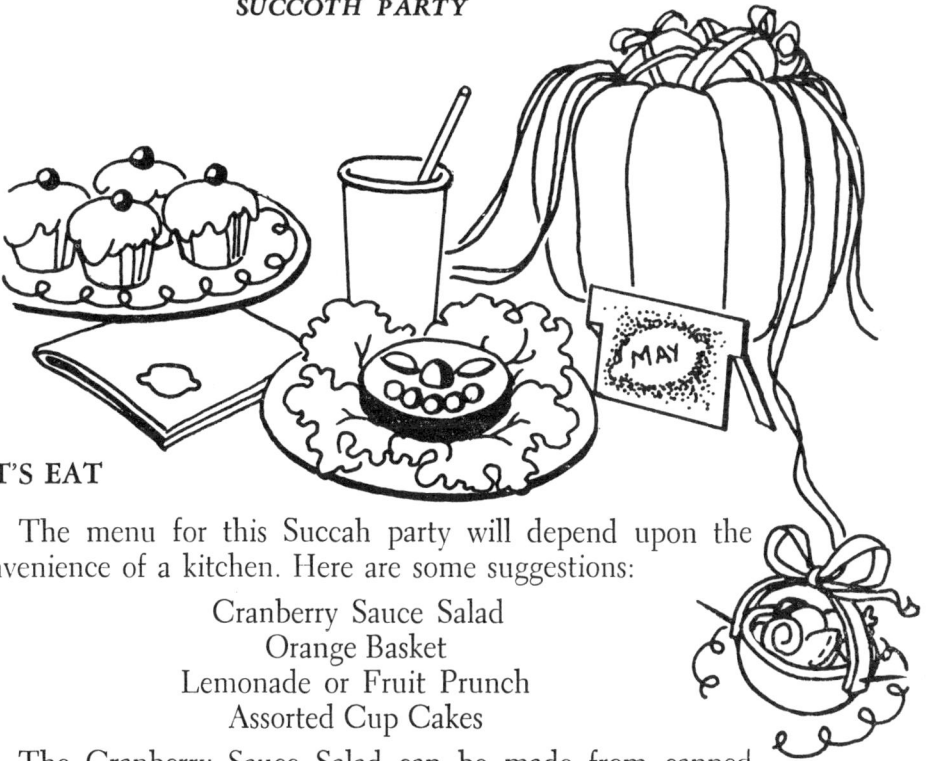

LET'S EAT

The menu for this Succah party will depend upon the convenience of a kitchen. Here are some suggestions:

Cranberry Sauce Salad
Orange Basket
Lemonade or Fruit Prunch
Assorted Cup Cakes

The Cranberry Sauce Salad can be made from canned jellied Cranberry Sauce. Cut slices about ½ inch thick and decorate each to resemble a face. Use two almonds for the eyes, a colored gum drop for the nose, and several seedless grapes for the mouth. Place this on a leaf of green lettuce.

Use one orange per child for the Orange Basket. Cut it in half and scoop out both halves. (The juice can be used in the fruit punch.) Fill one half with nuts, candy, etc. Cut a semi-circle strip from the other half and fasten to sides of filled half with pieces of colored tooth picks.

A FAVOR FOR EACH CHILD

Have a variety of small favors, one for each child. These may be a ball, a card of jacks, a whistle, etc. Wrap each one in tissue paper, attach a long colored ribbon and place in the pumpkin centerpiece on the table.

GAMES ARE FUN

1) I Visited My Uncle's Farm:

First child begins by saying; "I visited my uncle's farm and on his farm I saw a pumpkin." Second child repeats what the first said and adds the name of another fruit or vegetable. Third child repeats both and adds his own, etc. If a child omits something or gets the order wrong, he is 'out'. The last one left is the winner.

2) Here's the Way We Build Our Succah:

Children form a circle and sing to the tune of "Mulberry Bush." Of course, they supply the appropriate gestures.

> Here's the way we build our Succah, build our Succah,
>   build our Succah,
> Here's the way we build our Succah
> So early in the morning.
> Here's the way we saw the wood.
> Here's the way we hammer the nails.
> Here's the way we gather the greens.
> Here's the way we put them on the roof.
> Now our Succah is all done, is all done, is all done,
> Now our Succah is all done,
> So early Succoth morning.

3) Walking Race Around the Succah:

Divide the group into two teams. Call one the Lulav Team, the other the Ethrog Team. Give an apple to the first member of each. At a given signal, each first member starts walking around the Succah, one going clockwise while the other goes counter-clockwise. When Number 1 returns to his team, he gives the apple to Number 2 and takes a place at the rear of his team. Number 2 then has his turn to walk around the Succah as rapidly as he can. The winning team is the one whose members have all walked around the Succah first.

4) Exchanging Places:

Both teams line up facing each other. Give the name of the same fruit or vegetable to one member of each team. 'It' stands in the middle and calls out one of the assigned names. The two children bearing that name have to exchange places while 'It' tries to get into one of the vacated places. The child left without a place is the next 'It'.

5) Guessing Game:

Put several pieces of fruit in a paper bag, one of each variety. Let each child have a turn to close his eyes, put his hand in the bag, grasp one piece and call out the name. Then he lifts the fruit out and holds it up for the others to see if he guessed correctly. This is a particularly good sensory game for younger children.

6) Stringing Cranberries:

This activity is optional and is appropriate if the party is given during Chol HaMoed (the middle days of Succoth).

Set out bowl of cranberries, one bowl to be used by two children. Supply each child with a long tapestry needle and a long, strong thread. At a given signal, the children start stringing the cranberries. Stop them at the end of a few minutes. The child with the most cranberries on his string is the winner and should receive a token prize. The children might then hang up their cranberry strings around the Succah as added decorations.

THE PARTY FROM BEGINNING TO END

1) The guests find their places at the table and sit down.
2) Game at the table: "I Visited My Uncle's Farm."
3) Eat.
4) Story at the table.
5) Stringing Cranberries, if appropriate.
   At this point, the guests leave the table and hang their cranberry strings about the Succah.
6) An active Game for all.
   For the younger children—the singing game of "Here's the Way We Build Our Succah."
   For an older group—Walking Race Around the Succah.
7) Game of Exchanging Places.
8) A quiet Activity—The Guessing Game.
Home!

MATERIALS WE NEED FOR THIS PARTY

For the Invitations—colored construction paper, paste, crayons.
For Room Decorations—leaves, branches, fruit, green crepe paper, twine.
For the Centerpiece—large pumpkin, colored streamers.
For the Favors—a variety of small toys, tissue paper.
For the Place Cards—construction paper in pastel colors, soft black pencil, white paper.
For Stringing Cranberries — bowls of cranberries, tapestry needles, strong thread.

SIMCHAT TORAH PARTY

THE OCCASION

Simchat Torah is a gay, happy holiday when we celebrate our continuous joy in the Torah. It takes one full year to read the Torah in the Synagogue. On this special day, the last portion is read, and, immediately following the completion, the reading is started all over again from the very beginning. Young and old join in dancing and singing for this joyous occasion. The men carry Torahs and the children may carry flags.

A party for this holiday may be held either at home for a relatively small group of guests or in a Synagogue or community center for a larger group of children.

WE INVITE THE GUESTS

The invitation is in the shape of a Simchat Torah flag. Trace Figure 1 on to red construction paper. With black magic marker, shade the 'stick' and the edges of the flag and apple. Actually, any colored construction paper would do for the flag, but the apple should be red. Cut out and write message on one side and the information relating to the date, time and place on the other.

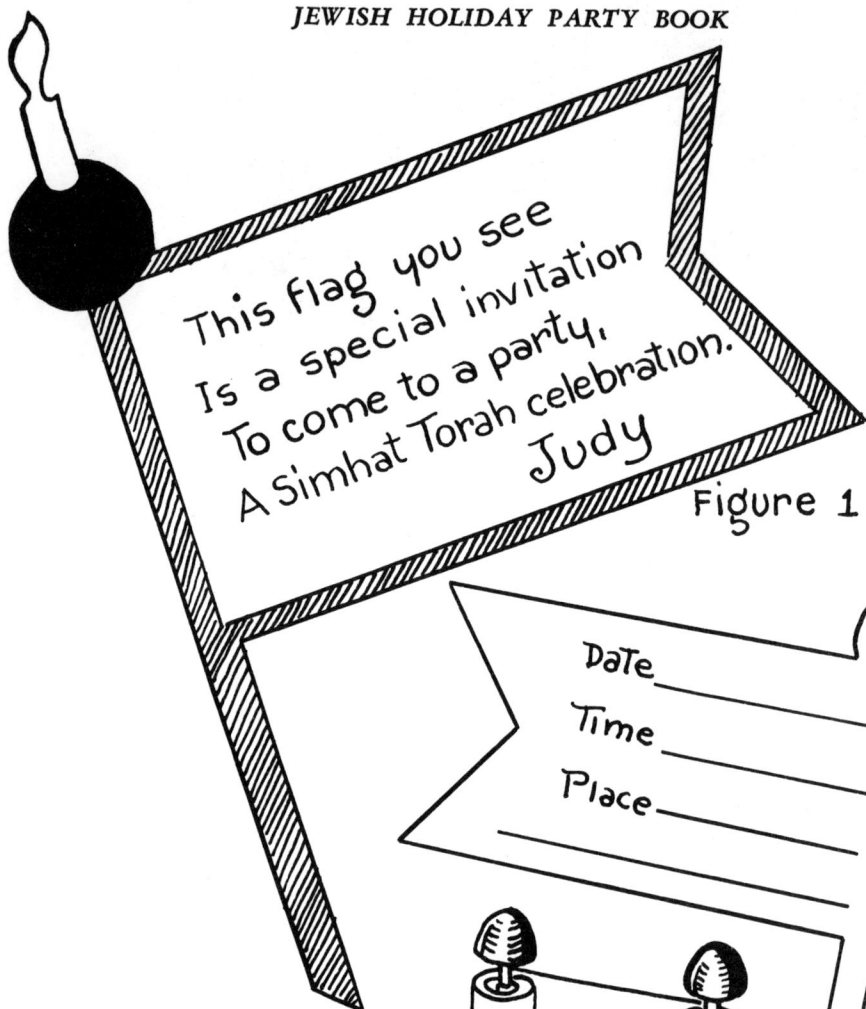

This flag you see
Is a special invitation
To come to a party,
A Simhat Torah celebration.
Judy

Figure 1

Date_____
Time_____
Place_____

Figure 2

WE DECORATE THE TABLE

The place card is in the shape of a Torah. Cut a strip of construction paper 2½"x9". With scotch tape, attach a lollipop stick or a 3½" dowel stick to each end of the paper.

Roll paper around sticks—towards each other. Cover four small gumdrops with silver foil. Put covered gumdrops on top and bottom of both sticks. See Figure 2.

For a centerpiece, use a wide-mouthed vase. Place Simchat Torah flags into this vase, one for each guest. Each flag may be of a different color and may be bought at a store that sells Jewish holiday articles.

TIME TO EAT

Suggested Menu:

Raisins, nuts, small candies in individual bags
Jelly Apple
Cookies
Soda

A FAVOR FOR EACH CHILD

Each child takes home a Simchat Torah Flag.

GAMES ARE FUN

1) Dancing with the Torah:

The children stand in a circle. One child is the leader and stands in the center holding a small Torah or a flag. Any holiday songs may be sung while the leader dances with the Torah or the flag and the children imitate him. The leader then chooses another child to be the leader. He hands him the Torah or the flag and he joins the circle. This can be repeated until all of the children have had a chance to be the leader.

Here are two simple songs that are appropriate.

TORAH ORAH

DUNDAI

La-la-la may be substituted for words after Dundai.

2) Bible Pictures:
Before the party, prepare about ten pictures, drawn or pasted on to construction paper. These pictures can be very simple but each one should tell some story that is in the Bible. Each picture is shown to the children. The child who recognizes the picture in connection with a Bible story, may keep the picture. The child who collects the most pictures, wins. Suggestions for pictures—a garden, an apple, a snake, an ark, a multi-colored coat, a baby in a basket, a slingshot, a giant, the Ten Commandments, etc.

3) Names in the Bible:
How many people in the Bible can a child name? Set a time limit of one minute. The one who names the most wins.

4) Who Am I?
One child is 'up.' He thinks about a personality in the Bible and is permitted to give a hint. The child who guesses is the next one 'up.' Here are some sample hints:

I'm very young but I can slay a big giant. (David)
Some people say I am the strongest man in the world. (Samson)
I lived in the time of a big flood. (Noah)
I hid in the bushes and saw the princess find my brother. (Miriam)

THE PARTY FROM BEGINNING TO END

1) If possible, a small Torah should be on display so that the children may look into it, and perhaps read portions or recognize some words in it.
2) Game: Dancing with the Torah
3) Game: Bible Pictures
4) Eat
5) Other games
6) Read a story from the Bible
7) Home

MATERIALS WE NEED FOR THIS PARTY

For the Invitations: construction paper, black magic marker, scissors

For the Centerpiece: a vase, Simchat Torah flags—one for each guest.

For the Place Card: construction paper, lollipop sticks or dowel sticks, Scotch tape, small gumdrops, silver foil.

For the Games: a small Torah or a flag, 10 simple Bible story pictures.

CHANUKAH

THE OCCASION

Chanukah is a joyous festival for children because all of its activities are so appealing. Chanukah 'gelt' and gifts are happily exchanged, the dreidel is spun amidst excitement, and latkes are eaten with relish. The lighting of the candles in the Menorah is a beautiful and meaningful ceremony. A good Chanukah party can include all these traditional activities and be cherished for a long time in the memories of those who participate.

Any one of the eight days of Chanukah is a good time to have this party.

WE INVITE THE GUESTS

The invitation to the Chanukah Party is in the form of a Dreidel, which is the popular name for the Chanukah spinner or top. When the handle is pulled out, the message can be read.

For each invitation, cut out 2 copies of Figure 1 from colored construction paper. Put these together by Scotch Taping all outer edges except the top. Cut out a copy of Figure 2. On this write the message as shown and then slip into the open top.

29

For the Time of the

HAPPY
CHANUKAH

HAPPY
CHANUKAH

Figure 1

For The Time of your life
And a day To remember
Come To my Chanukah
party
On The .... of December
Michael

FRONT

Figure 2

Address-------------------

Time..........................

Bring a small gift for
Chanukah grab-bag.

BACK

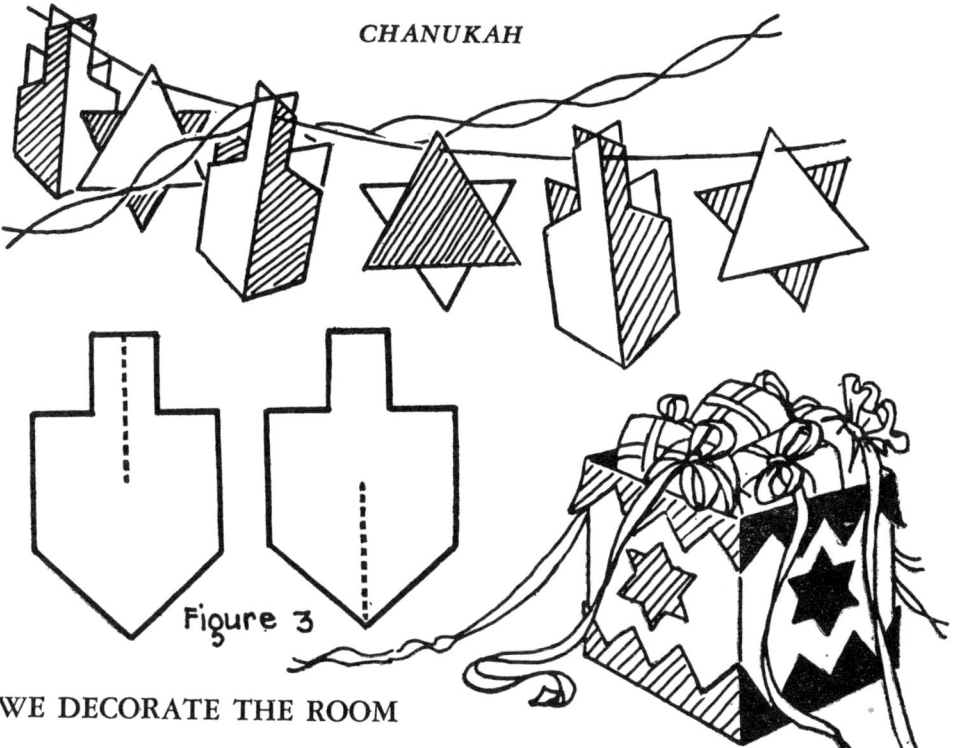

Figure 3

WE DECORATE THE ROOM

Let's have the party room festive and gay. Signs saying "Happy Chanukah" or with the Hebrew characters שמח חנוכה should be in evidence. Menorahs can be made from colored paper and taped on the walls. Colored streamers can be strung across the room from which can dangle paper Dreidels and Jewish stars.

Here is an easy way to make the Dreidel decorations. Trace the outline of a Dreidel, as shown in Figure 3. Enlarge to any size you desire and cut out many of them. Take one Dreidel and slit it halfway up, from the bottom. Slit another one halfway down from the top. Fit both of them together.

A Grab-Bag Box should be one of the first things each guest sees. Take a corrugated box and cover it with white crepe paper. Use light blue crepe paper for the trim and the Jewish star.

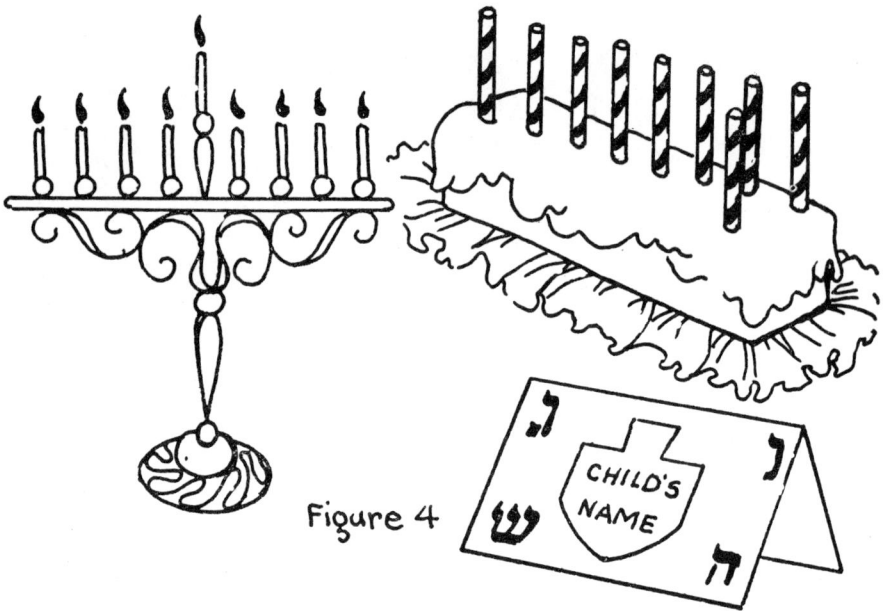

Figure 4

WE SET THE TABLE

The most appropriate centerpiece is a real Menorah with the correct number of candles for that day. A secondary center-piece could be a cake Menorah. This is a cake baked in a loaf pan and covered with chocolate icing. Insert peppermint or candy sticks into the cake, to resemble Chanukah candles.

In front of each setting, put a place card like the one shown in Figure 4. Make this from a piece of colored paper 4x6. Fold it in half so that it stands and trace the design on the front.

A small Dreidel box for each setting can be filled with candy and a new, shiny penny. Follow the pattern as shown in Figure 5. Use light-weight oak tag and fold on heavy lines. Fasten with Scotch Tape.

A plate with a Menorah Salad, as described in the next section, and a paper cup for a hot drink will complete the indivi-dual setting.

Figure 5

33

TIME TO EAT

Here is a suggested menu:

Menorah Salad
Potato Latkes
Menorah Cake
Candy in Dreidel Box
Hot Chocolate

To make the Menorah Salad take a roll and cut in half, the narrow way. Slice off the rounded bottom. Put cream cheese on top of each half. Into this put carrot sticks upright to resemble candles.

A FAVOR FOR EACH CHILD

Give each child a Dreidel when he first arrives and puts his gift in the Grab Bag.

At the end of the party, each child gets a gift from the Grab Bag.

GAMES ARE FUN

1) Dreidel Spinning Contest: The children start spinning their Dreidels at a given signal. Who can spin the longest? An easy Dreidel for young children to spin is a chocolate kiss with half a toothpick inserted in top.

2) Dreidel Score Game: There are four Hebrew letters on the Dreidel and each one is equal to a number. Nun נ is 50; Gimel ג is 3; Hai ה is 5; Shin ש is 300. Let the winning score be 1000. Each child gets a turn to spin the Dreidel and a record is kept of his score. The player reaching the limit first is the winner. Don't have more than four children scoring with one Dreidel.

3) Put and Take Dreidel Game: Each letter on the Dreidel stands for a word. Nun נ means nisht or nothing; Gimel ג means gantz or 'all'; Hai ה means 'halb' or 'half'; Shin ש means 'Shtel' or 'put'. Play this game with nuts, raisins, or small candies. Each player puts one into the kitty to start the game. As each spinner gets his turn, he has to do what the Dreidel tells him—putting, taking or doing nothing. Play until there is no more kitty and then start over again.

4) Hide the Dreidel: One child leaves the room and the others hide a Dreidel. He comes in and tries to find it. When he is close to the Dreidel the children sing loudly; when he is far away, they sing softly.

5) Passing the Dreidel: The children sit or stand in a circle. Play a Chanukah record and stop it at frequent intervals. The children pass the Dreidel quickly around the circle. Whoever has the Dreidel in his hand at the time the music stops is 'out'. The last one left is the winner.

6) Candle Tag: This is a very active game and requires more space, such as a basement or a hall. On the floor draw a Menorah with chalk. This is designated as the 'safe' area when the children play Tag.

7) Pinning the Candle on the Menorah: Draw a large Menorah and put it on the wall. Each child is blindfolded and gets a turn to pin the Shamosh or Leader Candle in its proper place. The closest one is the winner, the furthest gets the booby prize. Have a paper candle for each player; have him write his initials on it.

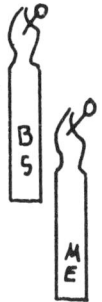

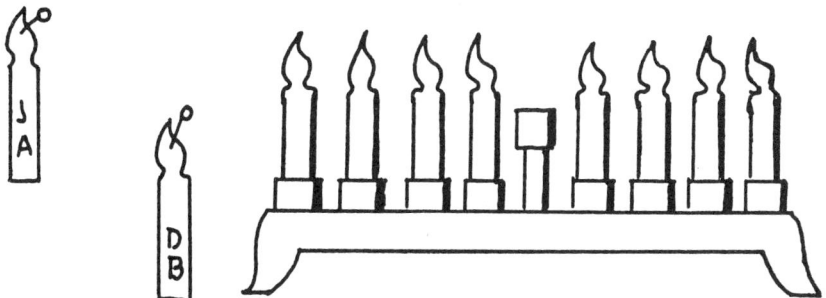

35

THE PARTY FROM BEGINNING TO END

1) As each guest arrives, he drops his gift into the Grab Bag and the host gives him a Dreidel.

2) Play a Chanukah record or two and also the Passing the Dreidel game.

3) Dreidel Spinning Contest. Bigger children can continue with the Dreidel Score Game.

4) Candle Lighting Ceremony. Light the candles in the Menorah and sing one or two Chanukah Songs.

5) Eat

6) Pinning the Candle on the Menorah. If the group is large, have two games going at the same time. The winner of each one competes.

7) Put and Take Dreidel Game.

8) Hiding the Dreidel Game.

9) Grab Bag.

10) Go Home.

MATERIALS NEEDED FOR THIS CHANUKAH PARTY

For the Invitations: Colored Construction Paper, Paste.

For the Grab Bag: Corrugated box, crepe paper in blue and white.

For the Place Cards: Cardboard or construction paper.

For the Dreidel Candy Boxes: Thin cardboard or construction paper. A new, shiny penny to put into each.

For the Room Decorations: Crepe Paper streamers, colored paper.

For the Favors: Dreidels—one for each guest.

TU B'SHVAT PARTY (Arbor Day)

THE OCCASION

Although we are in the midst of the winter season, this is the time of the New Year of the Trees in Israel. We can celebrate it here, too, with a gay party at which we partake of the fruits that grow in Israel. Indoor planting will provide a great deal of fun at this party.

WE INVITE THE GUESTS

The invitation to this party is in the shape of a leaf. Trace the outline of Figure 1 and cut out of green construction paper. Write the message in white ink. The day, the time and the address should be written on the back.

Figure 1

'Though its wintry in the U.S.A.,
Children in Israel have an Arbor Day.
They're planting trees 'neath a sky
of blue.
Come to my party and we'll plant too.

Larry

WE DECORATE THE ROOM AND TABLE

Have plenty of greenery around the room, such as vases filled with leaves and flowers.

Cover the table with a light-colored tablecloth and use the same color napkins. A border of trees all around the cloth, a large tree for the centerpiece and small individual trees for the place cards will express the significance of Tu B'Shvat.

The tree border can be made from regular green construction paper. Cut your sheets into three strips of 3x12 each. Take each strip and fold in half from left to right, then in half again, then in half once more. Now your folded paper should be 3x1½ inches. Trace the design shown in Figure 2 on to heavy oak tag or cardboard and cut out to use as a pattern. Place this pattern on folded strip with straight edge on left folds. Cut on dotted line as indicated in Figure 3. Open. Make as many strips as you need for a continuous border.

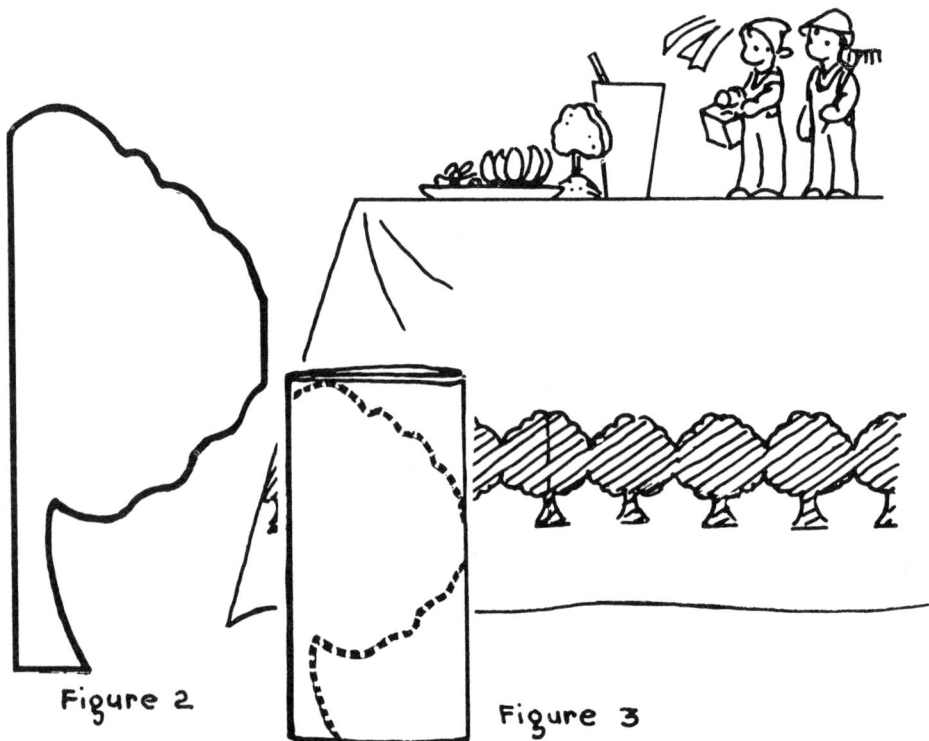

Figure 2

Figure 3

To make the centerpiece, which resembles a palm tree, take a large sheet of green construction paper, 18x24. Holding it the long way, crayon the bottom half brown. Roll the paper tightly. Cut strips about ½ inch wide from the top down to the brown. Curl each strip outwards by scraping the open blade of a pair of dull scissors along the bottom surface.

You will have to put the tree in a base in order to have it stand up. For this, you may take a shoe box and either paint it brown or cover it with brown crepe paper. Make a hole in the center, large enough for the roll of paper which is now the tree trunk, to get through. Invert the box and insert the paper tree in the hole.

Another kind of a base may be made from a strawberry basket. This, too, should be covered or painted. Make a hole in the center and invert it as directed for the shoe box above. Or, place the tree in the basket and surround it with plasticene to hold the tree upright. If you wish, you may attach pieces of fruit, such as figs or dates, to the paper branches with toothpicks.

If you have several small dolls, you may dress them in overalls or work clothes and place them on the table around the centerpiece so that they resemble planters.

For the individual place card trees, use plasticene for the base. Insert a dowel or lolly pop stick about six inches tall which has been sharpened to a point at the top. Get green sponge. Make a paper pattern of Figure 4. Pin it on the sponge and cut around it. Stick the cut-out sponge on top of a dowel stick and write the guest's name on the plasticene base with a toothpick. Look at Figure 5 for a completed picture of the place card.

A palm tree is made by slicing the sponge into ¼ inch layers. Cut this into strips about 2 inches long and ½ inch wide, tapering them at both ends. Stick strips of sponge on the dowel stick in criss-cross fashion, covering about one inch at the top of the stick.

If you wish to make a simpler place card, here is another suggestion. Make more of the trees which you have used for the table border. Cut out three full trees for each place card, by cutting off the two half-trees at the ends of each strip. Put paste on the back of the trees. Bring all the folded centers together and press firmly. This will make a three-sided tree. Write the guest's name across one tree, as shown in Figure 6.

Figure 4

Figure 6

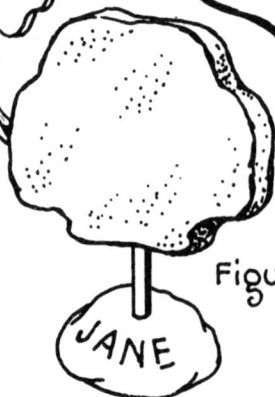

Figure 5

40

TUB'SHVAT PARTY (Arbor Day)

LET'S EAT

Israeli Fruit Salad
Fruit Punch

To make the Israeli fruit salad, take a seedless orange for each serving and peel it. Separate the sections down to about an inch from the bottom and lay it open on a plate covered with a paper doily. Heap some raisins and nuts in the center. Use a piece of carob fruit for the stem and two dates on each side as leaves. This makes an attractive and tasty dish.

A FAVOR FOR EACH CHILD

The favors taken away from this party will really be a part of the children's own activity. Each guest will take home something that he himself has planted. Before the guests arrive have small milk containers filled with soil. Also have a spray can ready. Provide the guests with things that grow easily, such as lima beans, radish seeds, carrot tops, etc. The children can have a planting session and take home whatever they planted.

LET'S PLAY GAMES

1) Guessing Contest:
Set up a bowl of almonds in advance. Next to it place slips of paper, a pencil and a closed box with a slot in it. Each guest picks up a slip of paper on which he writes his name and his

41

guess as to the number of nuts contained in the bowl. He drops his slip into the box. The one whose guess is closest to the actual number is the winner. Appoint a judge and have him announce the winner at the end of the party.

2) Paper and Pencil Games:

Give each child a pencil and a piece of paper on the top of which has been printed the word EUCALYPTUS, which is the well-known tree of Israel. Or you may have this word printed on a large placard to be placed in front of the group. At a given signal each guest starts to write as many words as he can find in EUCALYPTUS. The one who has 6 words first is the winner.

Now the papers are turned over. At a given signal, each guest writes down as many names of trees as he can think of. The winner is the one who has written the longest list of trees.

3) Chewing the String:

Pull a piece of long string through a fig so that the fig is in the center of the string. Or you may have it tied in the center of the string. Two children start chewing from opposite ends. The one reaching the fruit first eats it. Have several pairs of children chewing at the same time.

4) Nut Relay:

Divide the guests into two teams. You may assign names to them, if you wish, such as the Americans and the Israelis. In front of each team have a number of nuts to correspond with the number of members on the team. Give the first member of each team a teaspoon or a tongue depressor. At a given signal the first members push a nut each to the other end of the room or to a designated line. They then return to their teams and give their spoon or tongue depressor to the second members who do the same thing. The first team to finish pushing all the nuts is the winning team.

TUB'SHVAT PARTY (Arbor Day)

THE PARTY FROM BEGINNING TO END

1) Guessing Contest as each guest arrives.
2) Chewing the String.
3) Nut Race
4) Eat
5) Pencil and Paper Games at the table.
6) Have somebody tell a story for Tu B'Shvat.
   While this is going on in another room or in a corner of the same room, clear the table and cover it with newspapers. Then bring the containers filled with soil, the watering can, and seeds.
7) Planting session.
8) A judge announces winner of Guessing Contest and gives a token prize.
9) Children take their plants home.

MATERIALS WE NEED FOR THIS PARTY

For the Invitations—green construction paper, white ink.

For Room Decorations—leaves, flowers.

For the Table—cloth and napkins in a light color, green construction paper for tree border.

For the Centerpiece—a large sheet of green construction paper 18x24, brown crayon, dull scissors, shoe box or strawberry basket, brown paint or crepe paper, plasticene (if strawberry basket is not inverted), several small dolls dressed as planters.

For the Place Cards—green sponge, dowel or lolly pop sticks 6 inches long, plasticene, a toothpick.

For the Planting—Newspaper to cover the table, spray can, small milk containers filled with soil, lima beans or carrot tops or radish seeds, etc.

For the Games—a bowl of almonds, a covered box with a slot, small slips of paper, sheets of lined paper, pencils, long white string and figs, nuts for the Nut Relay, teaspoons or tongue depressors, a token prize for the Guessing Contest.

PURIM COSTUME PARTY

THE OCCASION

Purim is a jolly and merry festival. The Purim story is filled with exciting characters and events, and the traditional celebation of the holiday calls for gaiety, masquerading and noise-making. It has all the ingredients necessary for a children's party.

All children love to dress up. They fall in and out of character quickly. Purim is the perfect time for a costume party.

WE INVITE THE GUESTS

The invitation to this party is in the form of a mask as shown in Figure 1.

Fold a piece of pastel-colored construction paper in half and trace Figure 1 on it, making sure that the fold is the top of the mask. Cut along the outline, except top. Color in the eyes. Open and write the message as shown in Figure 2. On the back, write the specific information as shown in Figure 3.

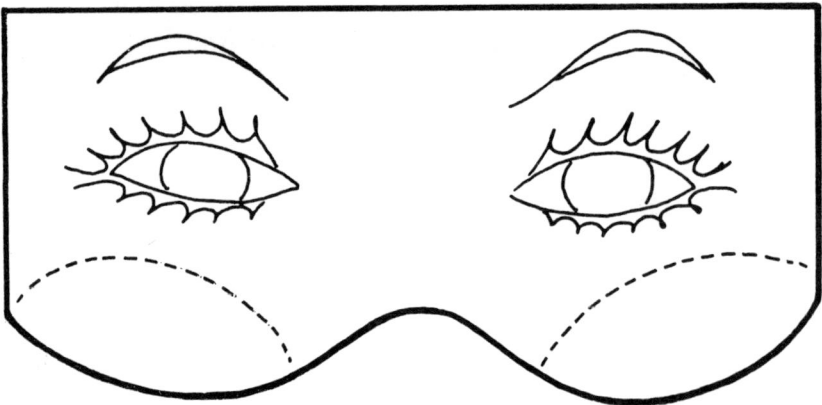

Figure 1

You're invited To a party
Which will be very gay
We're celebrating Purim
One week from this _____ day.

FOLD

You may come as Queen Esther
Or Haman, if you dare To.
Be a Spaceman or a cowboy
Or anyone you care to.

Rebecca

Figure 2

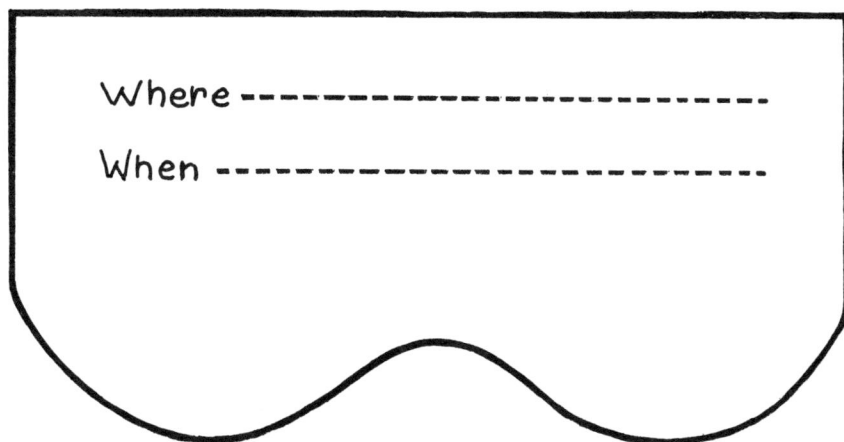

Where -----------------------------
When -----------------------------

Figure 3

WE DECORATE THE TABLE

At each setting put a place card in the form of a Megillah. Take a lollypop stick or a ¼ inch dowel stick, 4 inches in length. Use a piece of colored construction paper 3x9. Place dowel stick at left end of paper and Scotch Tape together. Roll paper around stick several times. Write child's name at right end of paper. Put colored gum drop on top and bottom of stick. (See Fig. 4.)

For the Centerpiece, let's have a Shalach Manoth Basket. Use any pretty basket or make this one. Take a brightly-colored sheet of construction paper in the 18x24 size. Fold in half and

DOROTHY

Figure 4

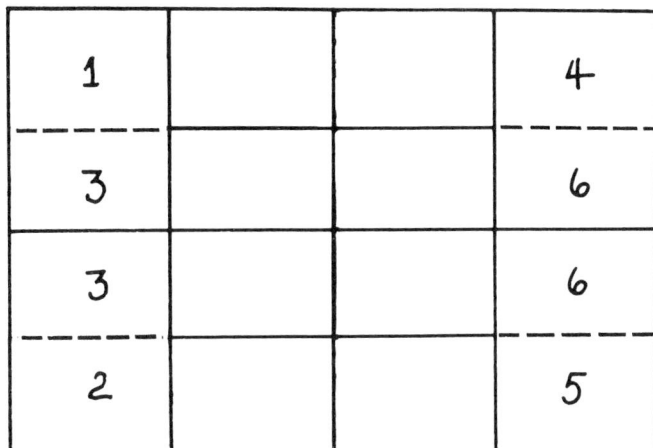

1			4
3			6
3			6
2			5

Figure 5

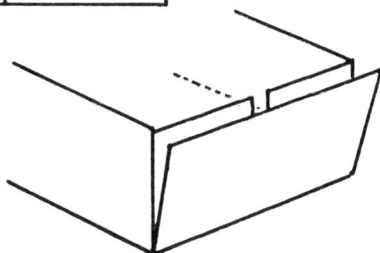

open. Fold the bottom up to the middle crease and then fold the top down to the middle crease. Open. Do the same thing, holding the paper the other way. Your paper is now folded in 16 squares.

Cut on the creases that are indicated by the dotted lines in Figure 5. Raise squares 1 and 2 and slide them together. Raise squares 3 and fold over the two end squares, 1 and 2. Scotch Tape together and do the same thing on the other side with squares 4, 5 and 6.

For the handle of the basket, take a long strip of construction paper about 1½ x 18 inches and paste or Scotch Tape to center of long side of basket.

Fill the basket with Haman Taschen, one for each guest. Cover with white linen napkin.

Each individual setting should also have a basket of goodies
in the shape of a Haman Tasch, a cup, a napkin, and a fork.

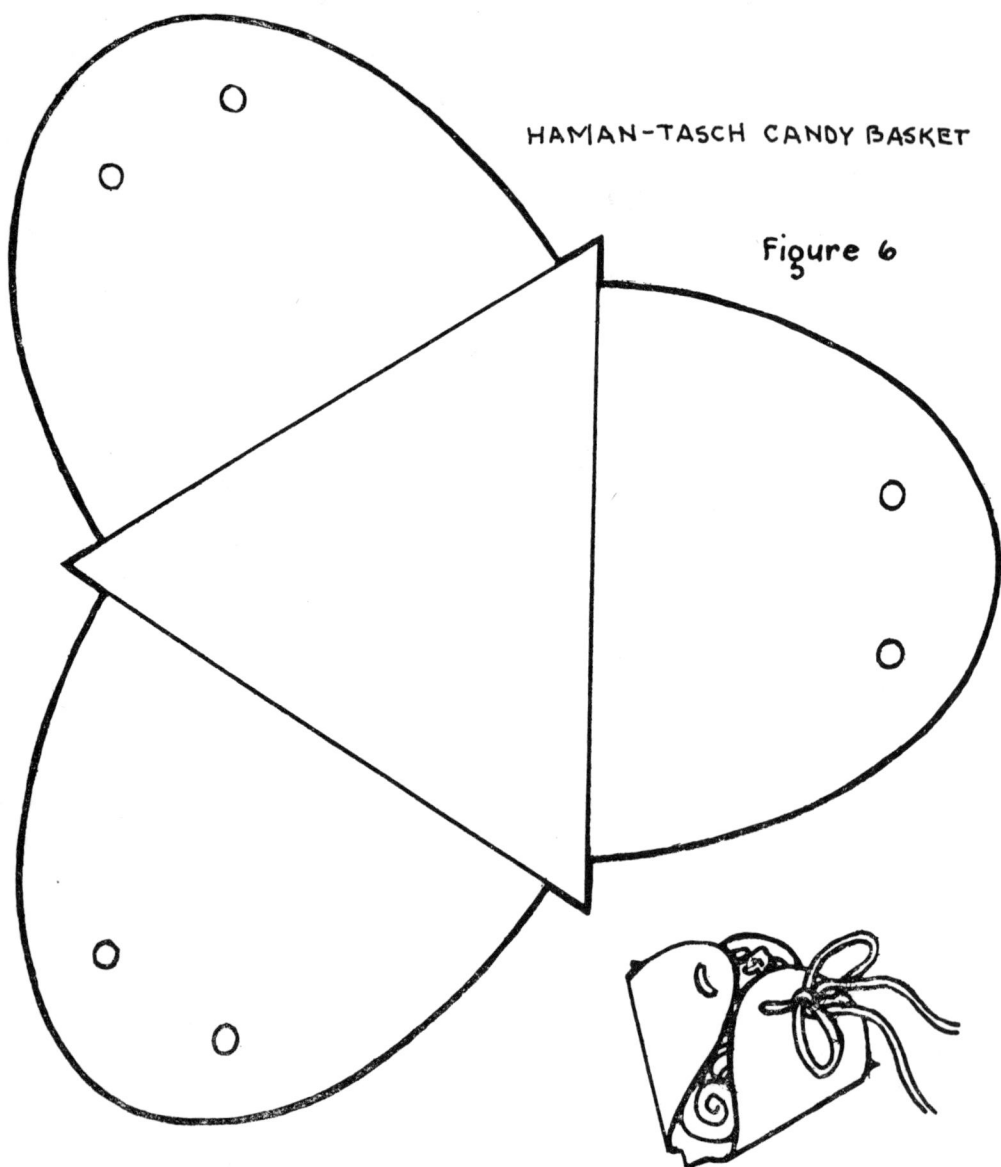

HAMAN-TASCH CANDY BASKET

Figure 6

To make the Haman Tasch basket, trace the pattern as shown in Figure 6 on colored construction paper. Cut out holes as indicated. Fold up on the heavy lines toward the center. Pull ribbon or colored yard through the holes and tie with a bow. Fill with candy, raisins, nuts, etc.

Small dolls, dressed as the Purim characters and placed on the table, would lend a decorative note.

TIME TO EAT

Suggested Menu:
Queen Esther Crown Salad
Candy Basket
Haman Taschen
Hot Chocolate

To make the Queen Esther Crown Salad, put a lettuce leaf on the plate and on this a scoop of cottage cheese. Take half a canned peach and cut 3 points in it. Place the peach on the cottage cheese and put red cherries in each point, for the jewels of the crown.

A FAVOR FOR EACH CHILD

Mask—At the beginning or the party, the host gives a mask to each guest.

Grogger—At the end, as each guest leaves, the host gives him a grogger.

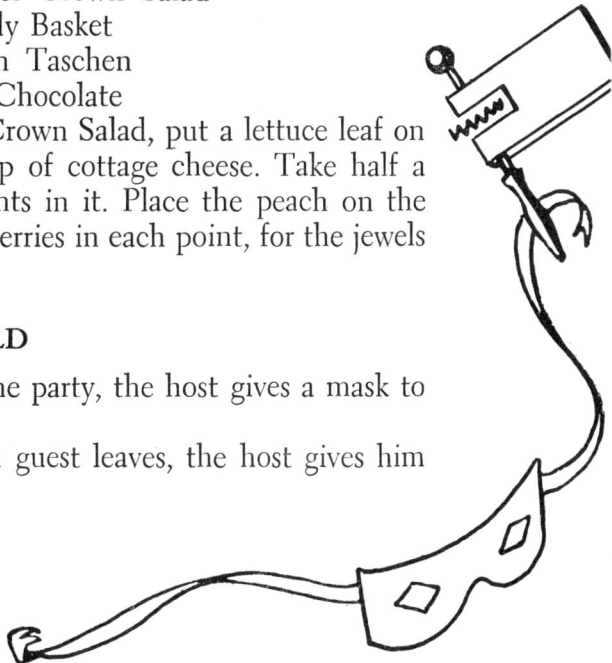

GAMES ARE FUN

1) Costume Game

Play a Purim record. Stop it at brief intervals and tap a child on the shoulder. He describes who he is and then asks the others to guess by saying, "Who am I?" If the children are very young, they may stand up and tell who they are and omit the guessing.

2) Hide the Grogger

One child leaves the room. The others hide a Purim Grogger and then call him in. As he tries to find the Grogger, the children clap their hands. When he is far away from the Grogger, they clap softly. As he approaches the Grogger, they clap more loudly.

3) Pinning the Tail on Mordecai's Horse

Draw a large horse similar to the one in Figure 7. Put this on the wall. Cut out tails and give one to each guest. Blindfold one guest at a time, turn him around three times and let him try to pin the tail on the horse. The one closest to the spot receives a prize while the one farthest gets a booby prize.

Figure 7

4) Purim Quiz

Here are some questions and answers. The child who gets the highest score in answering should receive a token prize.

1) What does the name "Purim" mean?
"Lots"
2) Who cast "Lots" many years ago and why?
Haman cast "Lots" to decide on what day the Jews were to be killed.
3) Who is the heroine of the Purim story?
Esther.
4) What was the name of Queen Esther's husband?
King Ahasuerus.
5) What is another name for Esther?
Hadassah.
6) What special book do we read in the Synagogue on Purim?
The Book of Esther or Megillas Esther.
7) Who was the enemy of the Jews?
Haman.
8) Who was Queen Esther's cousin?
Mordecai.
9) What is the name of the noisemaker we use on Purim?
Grogger.
10) When are the children supposed to whirl the Grogger?
Whenever Haman's name is mentioned during the reading of the Megillah.

THE PARTY FROM BEGINNING TO END

1) Host gives out masks as the guests arrive.
2) Play the Costume Game.
3) Eat.
4) Play the other games.
5) Tell a story, if you wish.
6) Dress to go home.
7) Host gives out Groggers as the guests leave.

MATERIALS WE NEED FOR THIS PARTY

For the Invitations—construction paper in light colors.
For the Place Cards—lolly pop or dowel sticks, colored construction paper, Scotch Tape, gum drops.
For the Centerpiece—Basket or large sheet of construction paper 18x24, Scotch Tape, white linen napkin.
For the Candy Baskets—construction paper, ribbon or colored yarn.
For the Favors—masks, groggers.
For the Games—grogger, large drawing of a horse without a tail, paper tails, two prizes.

PASSOVER FAMILY SEDER

THE OCCASION

The Passover Seder is a wonderful time for families to get together. Although this is not specifically a children's party, children can participate actively in the preparation for and in the entire proceedings at the Seder. The Festival of Pesach with the changing of dishes, the preparation of delicious foods, the eating of Matzohs, etc. is a very exciting time for the children.

WE INVITE THE GUESTS

If outside guests are to be invited, invitations can be sent out. Let this be in the form of the Hagadah, the special book read from at the Seder Table. Have this invitation open on the left side like a Hebrew book. Use one sheet of 9x12 colored paper for two invitations by cutting it in half. Fold each piece in half, then in half again. Cut the bottom closed edge, staple on right side and you have a 4-page booklet. On the cover, print the word 'Hagadah' as shown in Figure 1. On the next page, write 'Dear—.' On the next page, write a simple message, such as: 'Please join us at our Seder Table.' On the next page, write the host's name, the day, time and address. The children may decorate the covers, if they choose.

Figure 1

WE DECORATE THE TABLE

The usual Passover Seder table, famous for its dignity and beauty, is set. Place cards would add a bit of color to the table. These can be in the shape of flowers since Passover is also the Holiday of Springtime.

Use colored crepe paper or felt. Cut out circles varying in sizes up to 2 inches in diameter. Place several circles together, the smaller ones on the larger ones. You may fringe the edges, if you wish. Take a pipe cleaner and push it through the center of the circles so that about a quarter of an inch comes through the top. Bend top of pipe cleaner slightly to hold all the circles together. Twist bottom of pipe cleaner to form a stand. Scotch-tape a card with the guest's name to the stem of the flower.

GUESTS NAME

Figure 2

The ordinary facial tissue is a surprisingly good material for a flower. Take a tissue, preferably colored. Accordion fold it, starting at the narrow end and tie it at the center. Open the accordion folds out and separate the two layers of tissue. Hold the flower together, tie the base, and fluff out. Your flower should now resemble a carnation. Insert the pipe cleaner, as directed above, to make the flower stand.

The Hagadahs used at the Seder may be attractively covered in advance by the children. Let them make finger paintings in any designs. When completely dry, iron the paper on the left side with a cool iron. The children then fold the paper to cover the Hagadahs.

55

LET'S EAT

The traditional Passover meal is served.

WHAT CAN THE CHILDREN DO AT THE SEDER?

The Four Questions ("Mah Nish ta-nah")are usually asked by the youngest child. Any of the children may bring the pitcher or basin of water to the table for that part of the procedure which calls for washing of hands.

The children can hold the door open at that exciting time when Prophet Elijah is invited to come in.

But it is the 'stealing' of the Afikomen which is the highlight of the Seder. When the father breaks the middle of the three pieces of Matzoh, he puts away one piece and reserves it for the end of the meal. This piece is called the Afikomen. The children 'steal' this piece and hide it. They do not return it until they have been promised a reward. Since the Seder cannot be completed without the Afikomen, they are sure winners.

The children should be encouraged to join in the singing of the group songs at the table.

GAMES FOR PASSOVER WEEK

Nut Games are traditional at this time.

1) Which Hand? Child holds a nut in one hand but puts both hands in back. Another child has to guess which hand is holding the nut. If he guesses he gets the nut and has next chance.

2) Rolling the Nuts: Take an uncovered shoe box and cut out 3 holes of decreasing size. Give each hole a numerical value. Place the box on the floor with the open part down. Have the children stand behind a set spot and roll five nuts each, trying to get them into the holes. The child with the highest score wins.

3) Odds or Evens?

One player takes several small nuts into his closed fist and then asks another player, "Odds or Evens?" If the second player guesses, he gets all the nuts in the first player's hand. If he guesses incorrectly, he must pay a forfeit of the same number of nuts to the first player.

4) Pitching Nuts:

Place an open box or pan on the floor. Give each child 5 nuts. Each player gets a turn to stand at a starting line and try to pitch his nuts into the box or pan. The aim of this game is to get all the nuts into the pan. The child picks up his nuts that have not gone in and uses them again for the next turn. The first child left without any nuts in his hand is the winner and gets all the nuts in the pan. The game then starts over again. Make sure that each child has 5 nuts to begin with.

5) Nut Bowling:

Place a flat board, about two feet long, in a slanting position by leaning it against a book, box or other object. Place ten nuts on the floor some distance away. Arrange them in a circle or in rows of 1, 2, 3 and 4 nuts each, forming a triangle. Each player receives a chance to stand behind the board and roll a walnut down it, trying to hit the nuts on the floor. If he hasn't hit any nut, his remains on the floor. If he succeeds, he may take any nut that he hits and any others that are hit indirectly by his nut.

MATERIALS WE NEED

For the Invitations—colored paper.
For the Place Cards—colored crepe paper or felt or tissues, pipe
    cleaners, small cards, Scotch Tape.
For the Hagadah Covers—Finger paints and suitable paper.
For the Games—Nuts, Shoe box, pan or box, flat board.

ISRAEL BIRTHDAY PARTY
(Independence Day)

THE OCCASION

In 1948, on the 5th day of the Hebrew month of Iyar, the new State of Israel was born by the favorable vote of the United Nations. Despite the many hardships necessary to overcome in 'bringing up' a new state, the Jews all over the world were jubilantly happy. Every year we celebrate the Birthday of Israel.

WE INVITE THE GUESTS

Let the invitation be in the form of a Star of David. Take two squares of construction paper, 5 inches square, one blue and one white. Fold each in half on the diagonal, to form a triangle. Superimpose one upon the other in opposite directions so that the points are equally spaced. Punch 2 holes through the middle. Pull blue or white ribbon through and make a bow. Write the message as shown in Figure 1.

INVITATION

↕ 5 inches →

You are invited To a party
where we shall all celebrate
The birthday of Israel, a land
so great.

Date _____

Time _____

Richard

Place

_____

Figure 1

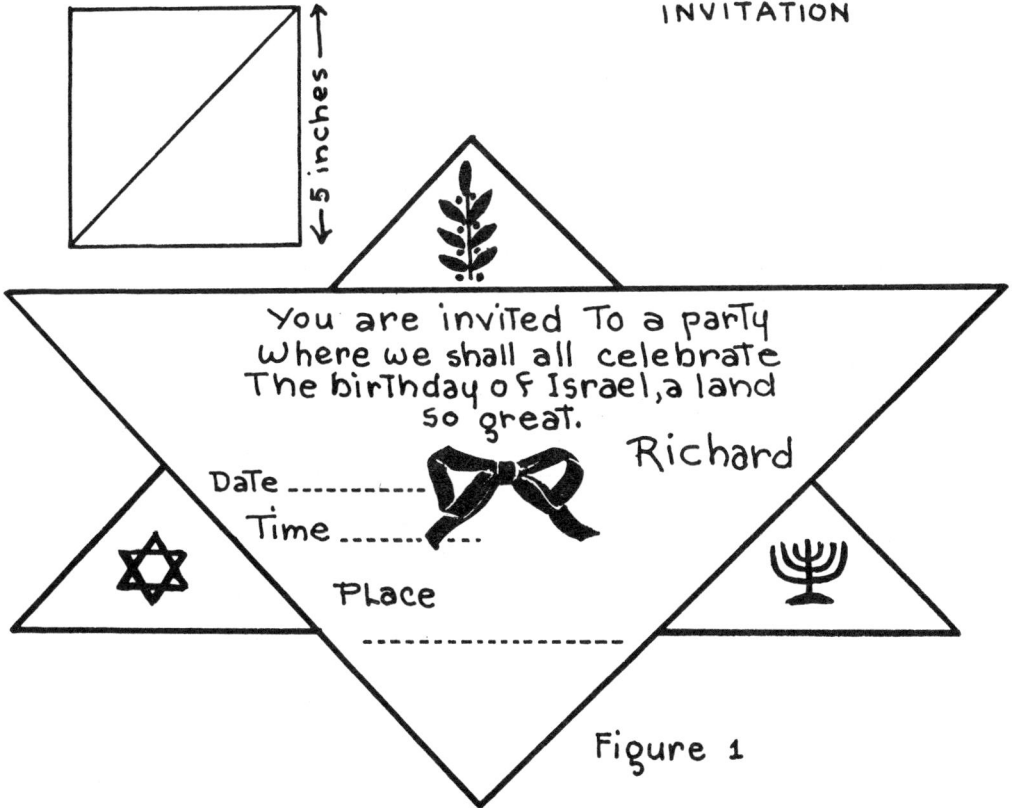

WE DECORATE THE ROOM

Have the blue and white color scheme throughout. Blue and white crepe paper streamers may be hung across the room and blue and white balloons attached to these.

Both the American and Israeli flags might be used as wall decorations. Make sure that the American flag is displayed correctly, according to law. The staff of the U. S. flag should be crossed over the staff of the Israeli flag and be displayed at the left of the crossed staffs. The U.N. flag should be displayed in a prominent place, too.

A picture of the Emblem of Israel, with its seven-branched Menorah surrounded by olive branches, could be shown. Pictures of Israeli scenes, personalities, etc., would add to the atmosphere.

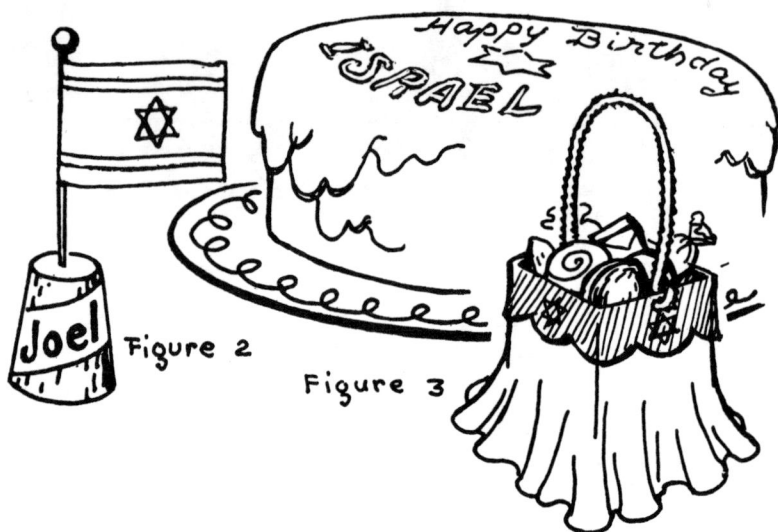

Figure 2

Figure 3

WE DECORATE THE TABLE

Have the blue and white color scheme here, too. On a white tablecloth stretch blue and white crepe paper streamers emanating from under the centerpiece. White napkins can have blue Jewish stars pasted on a corner. Use blue paper plates and paper cups.

The centerpiece, of course, should be a Birthday Cake. A white icing with blue birthday candles would be just fine. "HAPPY BIRTHDAY TO ISRAEL" would be the appropriate cake decoration.

The place cards for the individual settings can be simple and attractive. They are shown in Figure 2. Use a bottle cork for each one. Mount a small Israeli flag in the narrower end. Write the guest's name on a small strip of paper and paste on the cork base. The cork may be painted, if you desire.

Individual Candy Baskets, as shown in Figure 3, can be made in blue and white, also. Take small empty milk containers and cut off the tops. Cover the four sides with either solid blue or solid white crepe paper that has been doubled. Attach the folded edge around the top with Scotch Tape. Put a narrow strip of the contrasting color around the top to form a border. The outer skirt can be scalloped or ruffled or cut into strips. Colored stars might be pasted on the basket as further decora·tion. Now punch a hole in two opposite sides of the basket. Pull blue or white pipe cleaner through the holes and bend it to form a handle.

LET'S EAT

Here is a typical birthday party menu:

Birthday Cake

Ice Cream

Individual Basket of Candy, Nuts and Lolly Pop

Cold Drink—Soda or Chocolate Milk

A FAVOR FOR EACH CHILD

Inexpensive favors with an Israeli motif can be purchased. Pins, rings, key chains, etc., can be had with decorations of the emblem of Israel, or the Ten Commandments or the six-pointed star.

Wrap each in white tissue by placing in the center of the sheet of tissue and bringing all corners together. Tie together with blue ribbon or cord. Attach the favors to a ceiling streamer, having them hang at a convenient height so that the guests can reach up and snip them easily.

The balloons may be given away at the end of the party as added favors.

GAMES ARE FUN

1) Going to Jerusalem:

Place chairs in two rows, back to back, or in one row with each chair facing in the opposite direction from the chair next to it. Use one chair less than there are players. Have the players stand around the chairs.

Have somebody play Israeli songs on the piano or play Hebrew records. When the music starts, the players march around the chairs. When the music stops (stop the music suddenly) everyone tries to sit down in a chair. The player without a chair is out. One chair is taken away, the music starts again, and the players march again until the music stops. The winner is the last one to remain in the game.

2) Overhead Flag Relay:

Divide the guests into two teams, the "Blues" and the "Whites." Both teams line up. The first member of each holds an Israeli Flag. At a given signal, he passes the flag overhead and backwards to the other members of the team. When the last member receives the flag, he runs forward, takes the first place, and passes the flag overhead and backwards again. The team wins when its first member is back to his original place.

3) Paper and Pencil Games:

Each guest is provided with paper and pencil. See who can be the first to get five words of two or more letters from the word ISRAEL. Then see who can be the first to get five words of two or more letters from the word JERUSALEM.

Now, giving a time limit of perhaps two minutes, see who can write down the longest list of U.N. member nations.

4) Who Has the Flag?

Choose an "It" and then give a small Israeli Flag to one guest. He holds it in closed hands with palms facing. All the other children hold their hands the same way. The child with the flag goes from one child to the next, sliding his hands between the palms of each child. He drops the flag into the hands of one child without indicating whom. All the children continue to hold their hands in the same way while "It" tries to guess who has received the flag. The number of chances to guess should depend upon the size of the group.

5) I Took a Trip:

The first child says, "Last summer I took a trip to Israel and visited—." He finishes the sentence by mentioning the name of a place in Israel. The second guest repeats what the first said and adds a place of his own. Each guest repeats and adds. If a guest forgets a place or forgets the order, he is out. The last one left is the winner.

SUGGESTION

A new penny may be given to the winner of each game. At the end of the party you may suggest to the guests that they pool their pennies together and send them as a birthday present to the State of Israel. Have an envelope ready, addressed in advance to some generally approved organization affiliated with Israel.

OTHER ACTIVITIES

1) Hora Dancing:

Group dancing of the Hora, the popular Israeli form of folk dance, is loads of fun. The dancers can accompany themselves by singing, or play Israeli records. If the group, as a whole, is not acquainted with the dances, have at least one person present who can teach the simplest steps.

2) Movies:

If possible, get home movies or slides of Israel. Perhaps somebody in the community has visited Israel and has pictures with a personal touch.

THE PARTY FROM BEGINNING TO END

1) Before the guests arrive have the chairs set up for "Going to Jerusalem." Play the game and as each guest is "out," have him bring a chair to the table.

2) To the table. Light the candles on the cake and have all the guests blow them out together. Everyone sings:

> Happy Birthday to you,
> Happy Birthday to you,
> Happy Birthday, dear Israel,
> Happy Birthday to you,

3) Eat the refreshments and then play some of the games around the table. Play "I took a Trip." Follow this by giving out pencils and paper for the writing games.

4) Snip the Favors. The guests go to the area where the favors are hanging. Each stands in front of a package of his own choice. A pair of scissors is carefully handed from one to another and the guests have the fun of discovering what their favor is.

5) Play "Who has the Flag?"

6) Overhead Flag Relay

7) Hora Dancing

8) Showing of the film of slides. If this is done, it would be wise to curtail the time spent on Games mentioned in 5, 6 and 7.

MATERIALS WE NEED FOR THIS PARTY

For the Invitations—Construction paper in blue and in white, blue or white ribbon.

For the Room—blue and white crepe paper streamers, blue and white balloons, U.S., Israeli, and U.N. flags, Israeli pictures.

For the Table—white cloth and napkins, blue paper plates and paper cups, blue and white crepe paper streamers.

For the Place Cards — bottle corks, small Israeli flags, small strips of paper.

For the Candy Baskets—small empty milk containers, crepe paper in blue and in white, pipe cleaners in blue or white.

For the Favors—items with Israeli motif, white tissue for wrapping, blue ribbon or cord.

For the Games—sheets of writing paper, pencils, a tiny Israeli flag for the "Who Has the Flag?", 2 Israeli Flags for the Overhead Flag Relay, some new pennies for the winners, a stamped, addressed envelope, if you plan to follow the suggestion of a birthday present to Israel.

LAG B'OMER PICNIC PARTY

THE OCCASION

Lag B'omer, falling during the spring of the year, has become the time for outings and picnics. Since the days that Jewish scholars went out into the forests disguised as huntsmen to fool their Roman enemy, Jewish children all over the world have celebrated Lag B'omer by outdoor singing, dancing and playing games.

This is the perfect time for a picnic party. This type of party can be held in a backyard or a park.

WE INVITE THE GUESTS

The invitation to this party is in the form of a Target as shown in Figure 1.

Use 9x12 construction paper. Cut in half, using one sheet for two invitations. Fold each piece of 6x9 in half and trace the design of Figure 1. Make sure that part of the outline is on the fold. Cut this out around the outer rim leaving the portion indicated uncut.

Color each ring a vivid color. Open and write the message as shown in Figure 2. Sign the host's name and add the specific· information as to day, time and place.

Have your party start at an hour that will leave you sufficient time to reach the picnic grounds by lunch time.

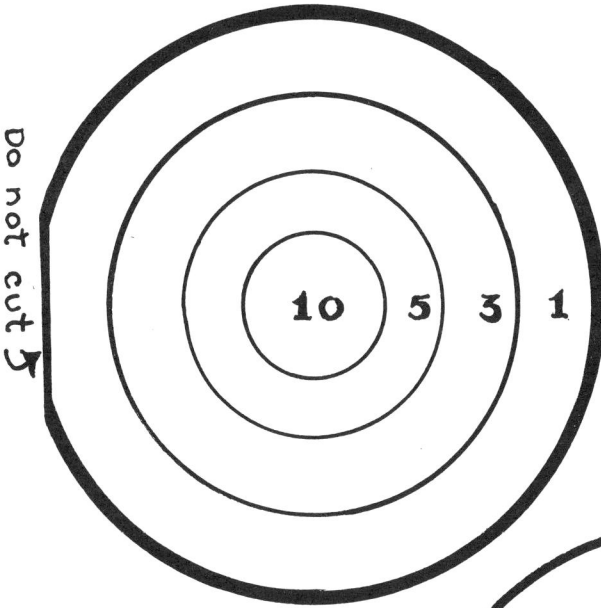

Do not cut ✏

Figure 1

10   5 3 1

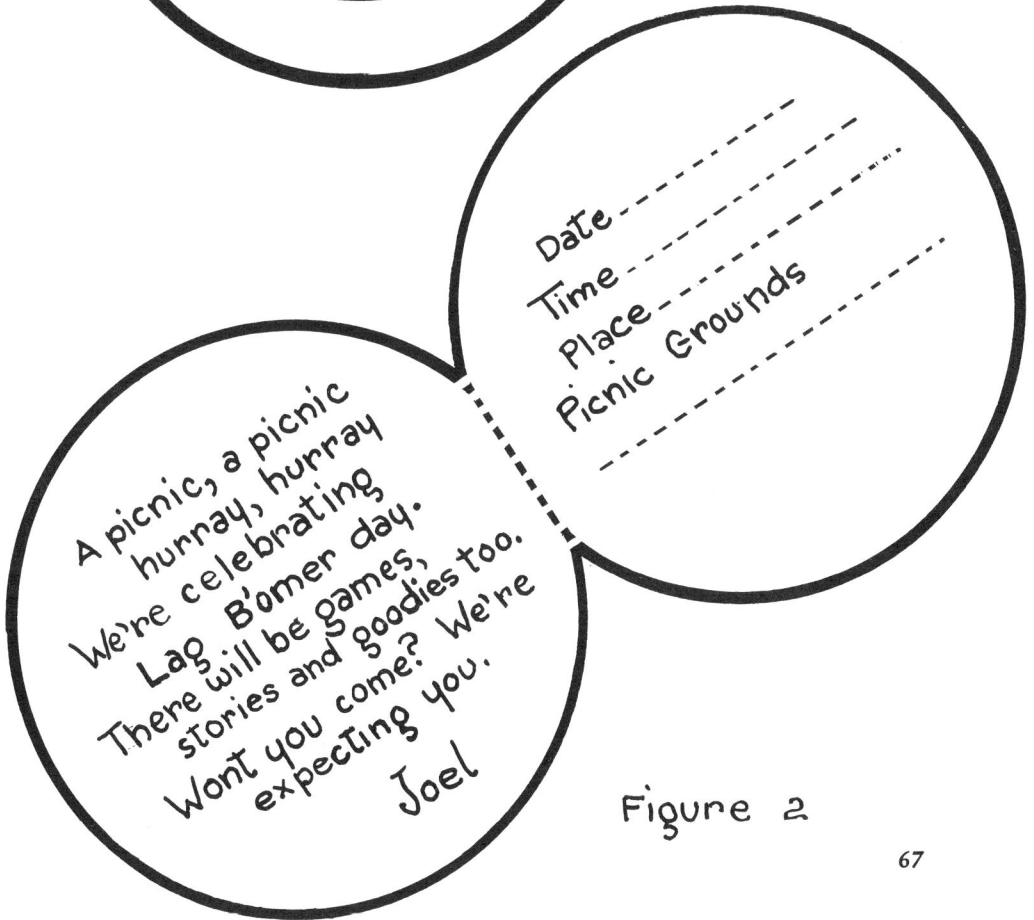

Date ----------------
Time ----------------
Place ----------------
Picnic Grounds ----------------

A picnic, a picnic
hurray, hurray
We're celebrating
Lag B'omer day.
There will be games,
stories and goodies too.
Won't you come? We're
expecting you.

Joel

Figure 2

WE DECORATE THE LUNCH PACKAGES

Get heavy paper bags, one for each guest. These may be used as is or decorated in advance. You may use crayons or paints for any simple design such as polka dots, stripes, triangles. Fill bag with lunch, making sure to include paper napkin and straw. After bag is filled, tie with blue and white crepe paper streamer. Attach card with child's name on to streamer.

LET'S EAT

Here is a suggested menu:

Sandwiches
Celery Strips and Carrot Sticks
Cup Cake or Cookies
Milk   Ice Cream

Each lunch bag should contain two sandwiches, a few celery strips and carrot sticks, and a cup cake or cookies. Serve the milk with lunch and reserve the ice cream for later in the afternoon. If necessary, arrange with an ice cream vendor for delivery.

For sandwiches, you might prepare cream cheese and jelly, or peanut butter. Salmon or Tuna Fish salad sandwiches are always popular, too.

A FAVOR FOR EACH CHILD

A kite, a bean bag or a ball may be given.

GAMES ARE FUN

1) Akiba's Students vs. The Romans:

Divide the group into two teams, giving each team the name of either 'Akiba's Students or 'The Roman's.' The goal might be` a specific tree. At a given signal, the first child of each team runs to the tree, returns to his team and touches the hand of the second child. The first one then goes to the end of the line, while the second starts running towards the tree. This continues until all the members of one team have had turns. The teaming finishing first wins.

2) Tap-a-Tree:

If the guests are up to the age of 7, they may not be ready for competitive or highly organized games like the Running Relay described above. Little children love to run but they cannot adhere to rules. They may play Tap-a-Tree.

Divide the group in two. Designate two trees as goals. At a starting signal, the children of each group run together, tap the tree and return to the starting point.

3 Follow Rabbi Akiba:

One child is selected to be Rabbi Akiba, the Leader. Everyone lines up behind him, copying everything he does. Switch leaders frequently.

4) Bow and Arrow Fun:

Attach a target to a tree. Give each child a turn with bow and arrow making sure the arrow is rubber tipped.

Older children may have an Archery Contest. The winner, hitting the bull's eye or closest to it, might receive a prize. If the group of guests is rather large, provide two sets of bows and arrows and avoid lengthy waiting for turns.

5) General Bar Kochbar:

This game is conducted while the children are sitting in a circle. One child, called 'The Roman,' hides his eyes until a child is designated as Bar Kochbar, the General. Bar Kochbar performs gestures which the others follow—such as clasping his hands together or snapping his fingers. 'The Roman' tries to guess which one is the General. When he guesses, a new 'Roman' is appointed and also a new Bar Kochbar.

6) Sending a Message to the Jewish Soldiers:

Children sit in circle.

The first child whispers a word into the ear of his neighbor who then whispers it to his neighbor. This continues until the last child announces the word out loud. If the one word is pronounced correctly, start a two-worded message. This can go on for several rounds, increasing the number of words each time.

THE PARTY FROM BEGINNING TO END

1) Wait until all the guests have arrived and then go to the picnic grounds. It is advisable to take along a few old blankets to sit on. Extra paper napkins and straws are alway useful, too.

2) When you arrive at the picnic grounds, it is a good idea to set up a marker to indicate where your spot is. A colored umbrella may be used for this. If a child strays, he can find his way back more easily by spotting the marker.

3) Play one active game, such as the running relay of Akiba's Students vs The Romans, or the Tap-a-Tree running game.

4) Have children spread blankets and sit down.

5) Give out lunch packages.
   Eat lunch and serve milk.

6) Play the quiet games of Sending the Message to the Jewish Soldiers and then General Bar Kochbar.

7) Give out the Favors.

8) Archery Contest or Bow and Arrow Fun.

9) Game of Follow Rabbi Akiba.

10) Serve the Ice Cream.

11) Tell a Story.

12) Pack up.

MATERIALS WE NEED FOR THIS PARTY

For Invitation:
    Colored construction paper 9x12.

For Lunch Packages:
    Heavy paper bags, 1 for each guest.
    Crayons or paints for decorating bags.
    Blue and white streamers.
    Small cards, about 3x5, for guests names.

For Favors:
    Select either a kite, bean bag or ball—one for each guest.

For Games:
    1 or 2 sets of Bows with Arrows and a Bull's Eye.

For General Use:
    Several blankets.
    An umbrella, for marker.
    Extra napkins, straws and cups.

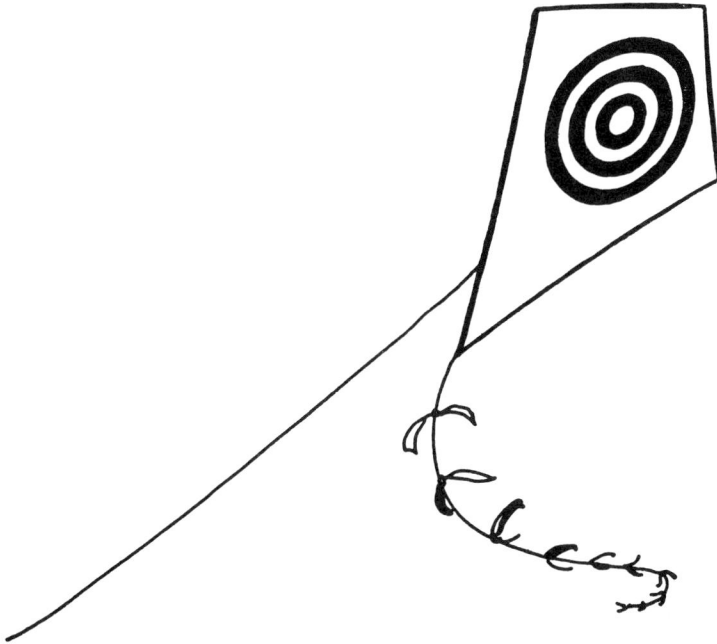

SHAVUOTH PARTY

THE OCCASION

Shavuoth is celebrated for two reasons. It is a harvest festival and a Torah holiday. It commemorates the giving of the Torah to the Jewish people and it is also the time for gathering the first fruits. In Israel, the children, dressed in white with garlands in their hair, happily bring fruits, flowers, vegetables to holiday ceremonies throughout the land. Here, in America, we decorate the home and the synagogue or temple with fresh flowers and greenery. Special dairy foods are eaten on Shavuoth.

WE INVITE THE GUESTS

The invitation may be in the shape of a Torah scroll. Trace Figure 1 on to construction paper and cut out. Write the message on the front of the card.

Come to the Shavuoth party
I'm planning for you.
Eat plenty of blintzes
And have fun too.
                    David

Date _____ Time _____
Place _____

WE DECORATE THE ROOM AND TABLE

The room should look gay and colorful, bedecked with green boughs and fresh flowers. Garlands of flowers can be made with paper tissue carnations as described in the Passover Seder. Using green string, tie the center of one flower to the center of a second and then to the center of a third, etc. The garlands can be placed on each child's hair or they can be strung up around the room.

The centerpiece may be a straw basket filled with fresh flowers, fruit and greenery.

A place card for each guest as shown in Figure 2, is made with colored construction paper or lightweight oak tag. A piece of paper 4x6 is folded in half so that it stands. Pin a souvenir Ten Commandment pin or pendant to the card and write child's name.

TIME TO EAT

SUGGESTED MENU:

Fruit Juice Drink
Crackers and Home Made Butter
Blintzes and Sour Cream
Ice Cream
Milk and Cookies

To make the butter, chill a pint of heavy sweet cream a few hours before the party. When the children are ready, pour the cold sweet cream into a cold quart jar that is securely covered. The children, sitting in a circle, take turns shaking the bottle until butter is formed. Transfer the butter to an attractive bowl and put into the refrigerator until ready to use. While the children are sitting in the circle and taking turns in shaking the bottle, they could be listening to records, singing, telling stories.

GAMES ARE FUN

1) Association Game:
   The leader calls out a name or place in the Bible. Each guest, in turn, responds with another name or place associated with the one called out. If correct, he stays in the game. If not, he is out. The last one remaining is the winner. In some cases, more than one answer is acceptable. Here is a list of suggestions:

Adam—Eve	Jonathan—David
Cain—Abel	David—Goliath
Garden of Eden—snake	Solomon—Wise King
Rebecca—At the well	The Temple—King Solomon
Daniel—The lions' den	Noah—Ark, flood
Samson—Delilah	

2) The Ten:
Who knows all Ten Commandments? Or, who knows more than any other child?

3) Arrange the Ten:
Write each of the Ten Commandments on separate sheets of paper, putting its number on the back. Mix the sheets. Ask for volunteers. The first child who arranges the Commandments in correct order (without looking at the back) wins.

4) Flower Relay:
Divide the children into two teams. Place three artificial flowers in a basket on the floor in front of each team. At a given signal, the first child on line of each team takes out a flower and puts it on a plate. He then goes back for the second flower and puts it on a plate and then the third. He then runs to the end of the line and the second child runs to pick up the flowers, one at a time, and puts them back in the basket. He then runs to the end of the line and the third child proceeds to take each flower out of the basket and so on until all of the children have had a turn. The team that finishes first wins. This game may be varied by having each child take the flowers out and return them to the basket before the second child starts.

5) Twenty Questions:
Two children go out of the room and decide on the name of a flower or a fruit. They come back into the room and the other children try to guess the object by asking questions. Only questions that can be answered by "Yes" or "No" may be asked. The first one who gives the correct answer wins.

SHAVUOTH PARTY

THE PARTY FROM BEGINNING TO END

1) Make butter
2) Flower Relay
3) Twenty Questions
4) Eat
5) Games: Association Game
6) Contest: The Ten; Arrange the Commandments in correct order.
7) Story: Ruth and Naomi or Moses on Mount Sinai
8) Children take Ten Commandment pin or pendant and go home.

MATERIALS NEEDED FOR THE PARTY

For the Invitations: construction paper of assorted colors.

For the Place Cards: construction paper or oak tag, Ten Commandment pins or pendants (can be bought in a store that sells Jewish religious articles).

For the Centerpiece: large straw basket, fresh flowers, fresh fruits, green leaves.

For the Room: green boughs, tissues, string.

For the Games: ten small sheets of paper for the Commandments, two small baskets, six artificial flowers, six small paper plates.

SABBATH AFTERNOON PARTY
(Oneg Shabbat)

THE OCCASION

The Sabbath, coming every week of the year, is considered to be the most important and basic of all the Jewish holidays. Many of its traditional customs and ceremonies are appealing to children—the kindling of candles by the mother, the chanting of Kiddush by the father, the special foods enjoyed by all the members of the family. Saturday afternoon's party can be enjoyed in the true atmosphere of the Sabbath.

WE INVITE THE GUESTS

The invitation will be in the form of the Ten Commandments. Trace Figure 1 on to light-weight oak tag or colored construction paper and cut out. Write the message on the front, as shown.

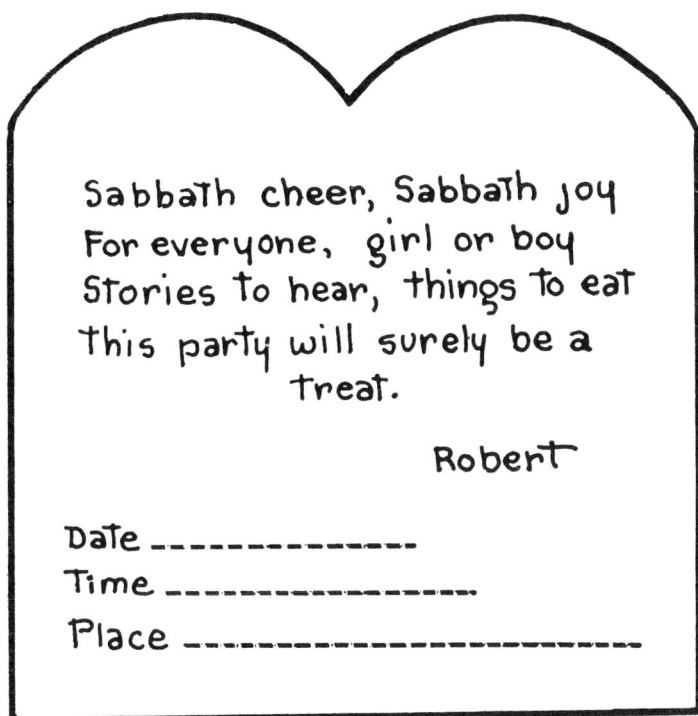

Sabbath cheer, Sabbath joy
For everyone, girl or boy
Stories to hear, things to eat
This party will surely be a
Treat.

Robert

Date _____
Time _____
Place _____

Figure 1

WE DECORATE THE TABLE

The table should be covered with a white cloth and have the Sabbath candlesticks as the centerpiece. On one side of the candlesticks, place a bowl of fresh fruit, on the other side a platter of cookies. A decanter filled with grape juice (to resemble a bottle of wine) can have a prominent place, too.

The place card for each guest can be made in the shape of a wine cup, as shown in Figure 2. Trace the outline and cut

Figure 2

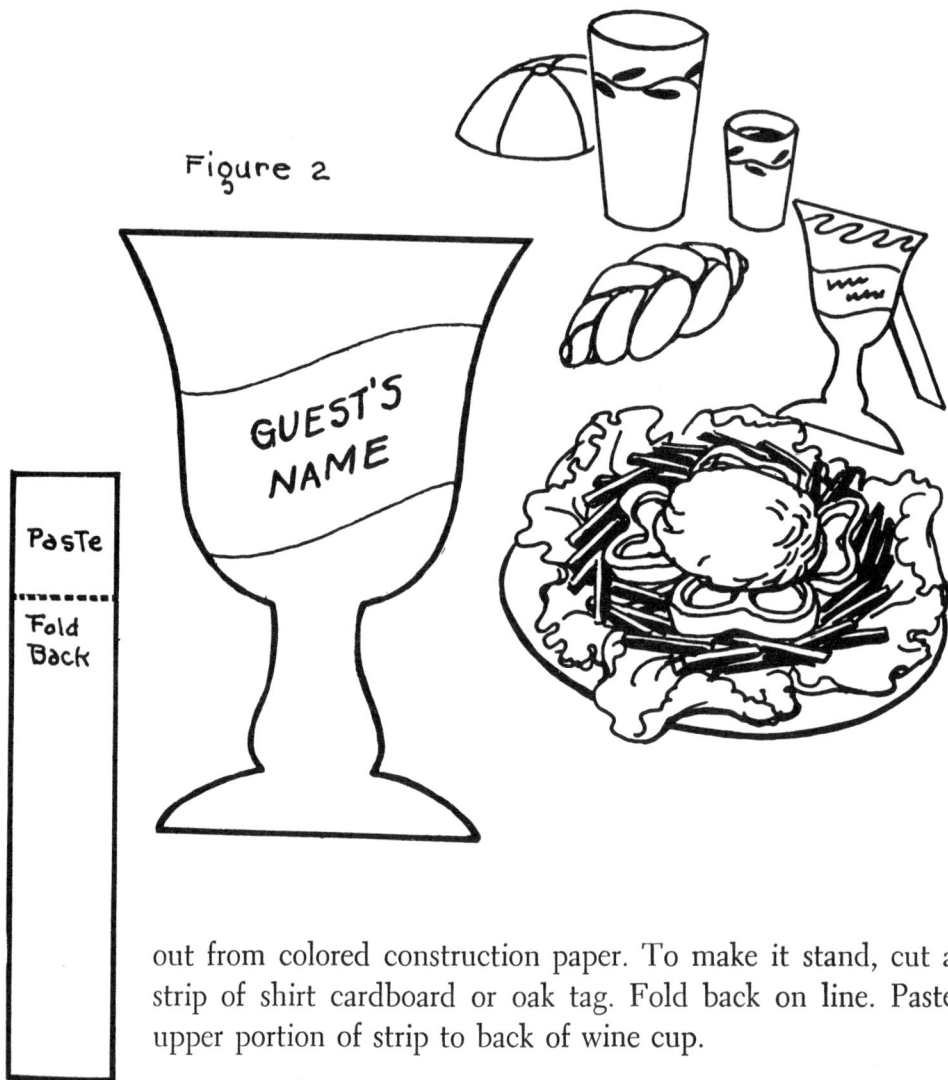

GUEST'S NAME

Paste

Fold Back

out from colored construction paper. To make it stand, cut a strip of shirt cardboard or oak tag. Fold back on line. Paste upper portion of strip to back of wine cup.

At each setting, put two paper cups—a small one for the grape juice and a large one for the soda. A plate with Geffilte Fish Salad, an individual Chalah, a fork, and a hat for each child (see Favors) will complete the setting.

LET'S EAT

Here is a menu that is very appropriate for the Sabbath:

Grape Juice   Individual Chalahs
            Geffilte Fish Salad
    Holiday Cookies   Soda

The Geffilte Fish Salad is both colorful and good to eat. Place a leaf of lettuce on the plate. In the center, put a portion of Geffilte Fish. Surround this with a ring of green pepper and an outer ring of beet strips.

Any cookies are appropriate to serve. For a more festive and completely Jewish atmosphere, cookie cutters in the shape of familiar holiday objects can be obtained at a Jewish Supply Store. Use your favorite cookie recipe.

A FAVOR FOR EACH CHILD

Give a Golden Crown to each girl, making her the Sabbath Queen for the day. The boys receive a fancy skull cap (Yarmulke). These are to be placed on the table at each individual setting.

The Yarmulkes can be purchased. To make each crown, take a 9x12 sheet of light-weight oak tag, fold in half lengthwise, cut points on folded edge as shown in Figure 3. Get a roll of gold-foil paper and trace cut crown. Paste gold foil on to oak tag. Attach both halves with two gold paper fasteners on each side.

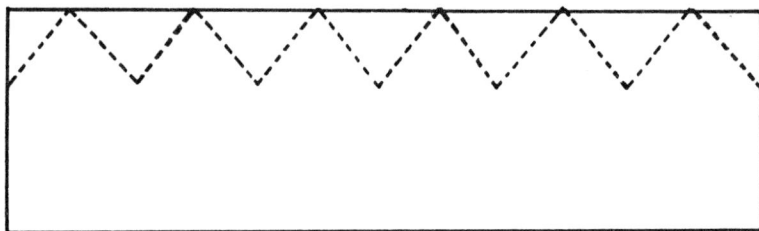

Figure 3

GAMES ARE FUN

1) Guessing who said "Shabbat Shalom":
"It" stands with his face to the wall. The leader silently points to a child in the group. This child disguises his voice and calls out "Shabbat Shalom." 'It' turns around and has two chances to guess who called out. If he guesses, the caller gets the next turn. Otherwise, he goes again.

2) Shabbat Buzz: Each player calls out a number in the proper order. Then the player who is supposed to call out number 7 calls out "Shabbat" instead (since the Shabbat is the seventh day of the week). When any multiple of 7 is reached— like 14, 21, 28—the person whose turn it is calls out "Shabbat." Also when the numeral 7 appears in a number like 27 or 57, the player must say "Shabbat." If he forgets he is out. The last player left is the winner.

3) Matching Halves: Here are seven sentences about the seven days of the week of creation. Take seven sheets of oak tag and print one sentence on each. Cut each sheet in two pieces in jig-saw fashion. Put all the pieces into a box and let the children pick one. The children try to match their pieces. When all the halves are fitted together, the children sit in couples. The mother or host calls out "First Day Couple!" Those 2 stand up and read their sentence together. This continues until the Sabbath or 7th day has been completed.

   1) On the first day there was light.
   2) The sky appeared on the second day.
   3) On the third day there were trees and grass.
   4) The sun and moon were created on the fourth day.
   5) The fish swam in the water and the birds flew in the air on the fifth day.
   6) The animals of the land were created on the sixth day.
   7) The seventh day is called the Sabbath.

4) What Flies? The leader of this game should be an adult. He calls out different objects followed by the word "flies," such as, "A bird flies," or "A chair flies." If the statement is true, the children are to raise right hand with index finger pointed upwards. If the statement is false, hand remains on lap. If child raises his hand at the wrong time, he is out.

5) Beast, Bird, or Fish: Leader calls out one of these categories, points to a child and counts up to 10. Child has to name one species within that time. No repetitions are allowed. If he fails, he's out. Last one left is winner.

THE PARTY FROM BEGINNING TO END

1) Matching Halves Game for the older children.
2) Who Said "Shabbat Shalom" game. Younger children can start here.
3) To the Table. Boys put on their skull caps and the girls their crowns.

  * Chant the blessing for wine and drink the grape juice.
 ** Say the Blessing for Bread and eat the small Chalah.

4) The meal follows.
5) Group singing of several Sabbath songs or well-known Synagogue songs, like Ain K'elohenu or Adon Olom.
6) Play the game of Shabbat Buzz at the table.
7) The other games may be played at the table or in another
   place.
8) End this party with a Sabbath Story told by an adult.

  * Boruch Ato Adonoy Elohenu Melech ho-olom, borey p'ri
   ha-gofen.
   Blessed art Thou, O Lord, our God, Who hast created the
   fruit of the vine.

** Boruch Ato Adonoy Elohenu Melech ho-olom ha-motzi
   lechem min ha'aretz.
   Blessed art Thou, O Lord, our God, King of the Universe,
   Who brings forth bread from the earth.

MATERIALS WE NEED FOR THIS PARTY

For the Invitations—colored construction paper or light-weight
    oak tag.
For the Table—white cloth and napkins, Sabbath candlesticks,
  decanter of grape juice.
For the Place Cards—colored construction paper, cardboard or
    oak tag.
For the Favors—Yarmulkes (Skull caps), oak tag, gold-foil
paper, paper fasteners in gold color.
For the Games—seven sheets of paper for "Matching Halves."

ROSH CHODESH PARTY
(New Moon)

THE OCCASION

The Jewish month is a lunar month, based upon the time it takes for the moon to make one complete revolution around the earth. The time amounts to twenty-nine and one-half days. We, therefore, count one month of twenty-nine days and the following month of thirty days.

Special prayers for the new month are said on the Sabbath immediately preceding the start of the new month as well as on the day itself. In connection with this event, it has been customary to go out into the open air and bless the new moon when it becomes visible. The people exchange greetings and wish each other good fortune for the coming month.

A Rosh Chodesh party may be given between the fourth and eleventh day of the new Hebrew month for that is when the new moon would be visible. The party should be held in the evening, as the main activity would be the observation of the new moon.

WE INVITE THE GUESTS

The invitation is in the form of the new moon. Using blue construction paper, cut out the circle, Figure 1. Using white construction paper, cut out the crescent, Figure 2. Paste Fig. 2 on to Fig. 1 as illustrated in Figure 3. Write message on blue paper with white ink. The date, time, etc. may be written on the back of the invitation.

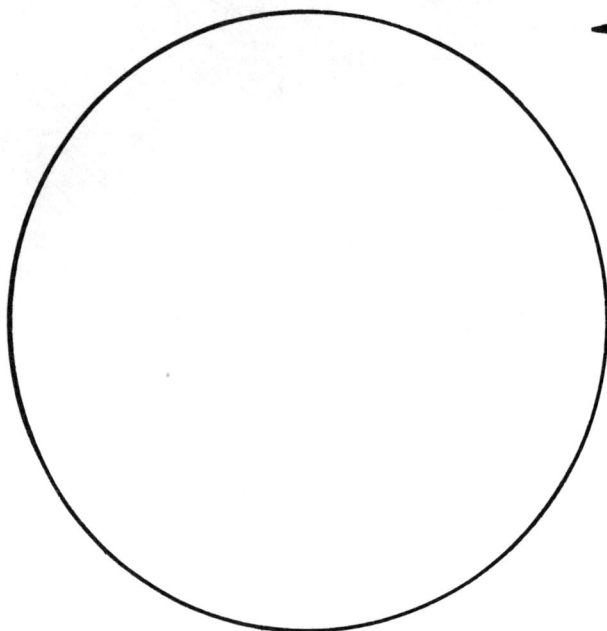

Figure 1

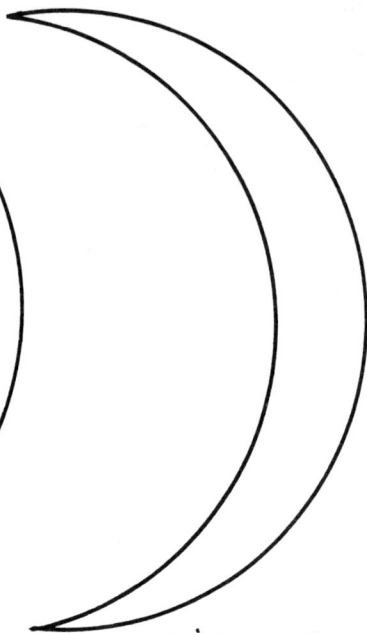

Figure 2

Let's have a party
On_____night
To greet the new moon
As it comes into sight

Adelle

Figure 3

WE DECORATE THE ROOM AND THE TABLE

Instead of putting a centerpiece on the table, make a "moonmobile" which will be suspended from the chandelier directly over the center of the table. If there is no available chandelier, string a streamer across the ceiling and suspend mobile from it. Using white, yellow and orange construction paper, cut out full moons, half-moons, crescent moons, stars, etc. Attach these to a wire hanger using varied lengths of string.

About a week before the party is scheduled, collect small snapshots of each guest. A "man-in-the-moon" place card can be made in the shape of a full moon with a picture of the child's face in the center. Each guest will know where his place is at the table by looking for his picture.

Fold a 6"x4½" piece of blue construction paper in half. Paste the guest's picture in the center of the front (Figure 1). Trace Figure 2 on white or pale yellow construction paper or silver foil. Cut out edge and center. Paste this moon frame around the picture. Paste small silver stars on the blue background.

Figure 1

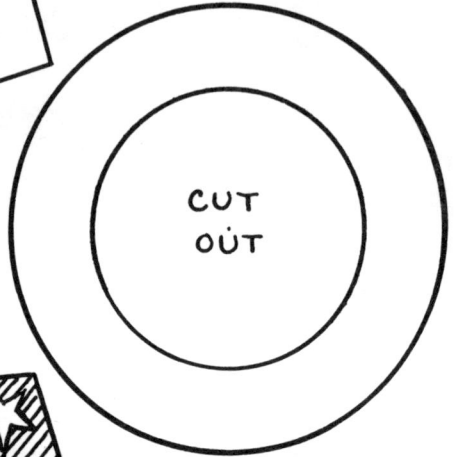

CUT
OUT

Figure 2

Figure 3

Decorate the room with inflated white, yellow or orange balloons. Hang up appropriate pictures of the solar system, spaceships, space men, etc.

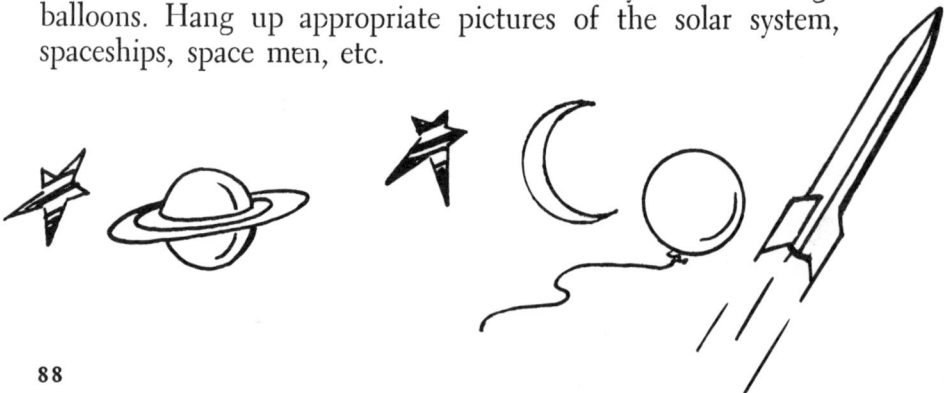

LET'S EAT

Suggested Menu:

Since this is an evening party, the fare may be as simple or as elaborate as desired. It may be a supper party, with a full meal served:

Fruit Juice
Hamburger on Bun
French Fried Potatoes
Soda

Or, it may be a dessert party:
Cookies—in moon and star shapes
Soda

A FAVOR FOR EACH CHILD

Each child may take home the balloon which he has decorated for the game "Keep the Moon Up in the Sky."

GAMES ARE FUN

1) Count the Stars in the Sky:

On a large piece of dark blue construction paper, paste a large number of silver stars, counting as you do so. As each guest enters, he is asked to study the 'sky' and to guess how many stars there are. On a slip of paper, he writes his name and answer. The one whose guess is closest to the correct number is the winner. The winner is announced at the end of the party.

2) Feed the Man-in-the-Moon:

On the back of a white or yellow paper plate, draw a face. Cut a hole for the open mouth. Hang the plate in the doorway by a string attached to the top of the plate. The children take turns throwing a Ping-pong ball into the man-in-the-moon's mouth.

3) Keep the Moon Up in the Sky:
Each child is given an inflated balloon and a magic marker. He then decorates it to resemble the moon (a face or anything which his scientific background dictates). He should put his name or initials on the reverse side to avoid confusion. At a given signal, the children throw their 'moons' up in the air and try to keep them up by blowing only. No hands allowed. The one whose 'moon' stays up the longest is the winner.

4) Put the Full Moon in Its Place:
Make a large calendar for the New Hebrew month being celebrated. Mark the fifteenth day with a large full moon and hang the calendar on the wall. Prepare yellow circles, preferably of gummed paper, and put each child's initials on a circle. Blindfold one child at a time, give him his 'moon' and let him try to place it in its proper place. The one who comes nearest is the winner.

5) Continue the Story:
One child starts a story about a landing on the moon or an adventure in outerspace. Each child continues the story.

6) How Many Words Can You Find?
Supply each child with paper and pencil. At the top of the page he is to write ASTRONOMER or ROSH CHODESH. Who can find the most words of two or more letters in a period of five minutes? Or, who is the first to get ten words?

7) Seeing the New Moon:
Everyone goes outdoors, looks upward and tries to find the crescent of the new moon. They exchange greetings:

"Shalom Aleichem, peace be with you!"
"Aleichem Shalom, peace be unto you!"
"Mazal Tov, may you have good fortune!"

If a telescope is available, the children would certainly enjoy looking through it.

A special quiz for this party:

Depending upon the age of the participants, questions may be selected from this list or simplified. Divide the children into two teams and have a contest. The team answering the most questions, wins.

1. What does Rosh Chodesh mean?
   Ans. The beginning of the month.

2. What is a lunar calendar?
   Ans. One that is based on the moon.

3. What is a solar calendar?
   Ans. One that is based on the sun.

4. Is the Hebrew calendar lunar or solar?
   Ans. Lunar

5. Is the American calendar lunar or solar?
   Ans. Solar

6. Does the Moon go around the Earth or does the Earth go around the Moon?
   Ans. The Moon goes around the Earth.

7. When is there a full moon?
   Ans. In the middle of the Hebrew month.

8. How long is the Hebrew month?
   Ans. Twenty-nine or thirty days.

9. Is the Earth a planet, star or satellite?
   Ans. A planet.

10. Is the Moon a planet, star or satellite?
    Ans. A satellite.

11. Is the sun a planet, star or satellite?
    Ans. A star.

12. Name a planet besides Earth.
    Ans. for questions 12-19: Mercury, Venus, Mars, Jupiter, Saturn, Uranus, Neptune, Pluto.

20. Which is the biggest planet?
Ans. Jupiter.

21. Which is the smallest planet?
Ans. Mercury.

22. Which planets are closest to Earth?
Ans. Mars and Venus.

THE PARTY FROM BEGINNING TO END

1) Guessing game. As each guest arrives, he "counts the number of stars in the sky."
2) Games: Put the Full Moon in its Place. Feed the Man-in-the-Moon.
3) The special quiz for the older children.
4) Supper
5) Continue the Story
6) How Many Words Can You Find?
7) Keep the Moon Up in the Sky
8) Story to be told by adults. Suggestion: The Helmites Capture the Moon, (*Wise Men of Helm* by Solomon Simon)
9) Outdoors to see the new moon.
10) Home

MATERIALS WE NEED FOR THIS PARTY

For the Invitation: blue and white construction paper, paste, scissors, white ink.

For the Room and Centerpiece: balloons, wire hanger, silverfoil, string, orange, white, yellow construction paper.

For the Place Cards: snapshot of each guest, colored construction paper, gummed stars.

For the Games: large piece of blue construction paper, stars, paper, pencils, paper plate, ping-pong balls, balloons, yellow gummed circles, magic markers, telescope.

MAKING PARTY HATS

Party Hats lend a note of gaiety and festivity to celebrations. Here are several simple methods of making a basic hat which may then be varied in numerous ways to blend in with the specific holiday.

Take a standard roll of colored crepe paper, which is 20 inches wide. Remove the wrapping but do not unroll. Cut through the middle, making 2 rolls, each 10 inches wide. Open one roll and cut off about 21 inches, which is usually a good length for fitting around a child's head. Fold up about one inch along the bottom, to make a firmer brim. Staple both narrow ends together and yon now have a basic hat.

By drawing the crepe paper together at the very top and stapling, you will get a pointed hat. Or, draw the paper together about 2 inches from the top and tie it there with a colored ribbon or string. If you wish to make the hat a bit more elaborate, take some contrasting paper, cut it into strips and insert in the top before drawing together.

A paper bag of a size to fit on a child's head may also be used as a hat. Fold it up an inch or two to give it a more definite brim.

A 12x18 sheet of colored construction paper may be rolled into a cone shape and stapled together to give a hat.

Any of the above basic hats may be decorated with colored circles, squares or other shapes which the child may paste on.

Designs appropriate to a particular holiday may be added, e.g. apple or Shofar for Rosh Hashanah, fruits for Succoth, candle or dreidel for Chanukah, grogger or mask for Purim, green leaves for Tu B'shvat, moon and stars for Rosh Chodesh, etc.

94

GLOSSARY

Afikomen   Piece of Matzoh set aside to be eaten at the end of the Seder.

Akiba   Famous Rabbi who started to study at the age of forty.

Bar Kochbar   Jewish hero who lead the rebellion against Rome in the second century.

Blintzes   Rolled pancakes, usually filled with cheese, eaten on Shavuoth.

Chalah   Sabbath or holiday bread.

Chanukah   Feast of Lights or Dedication, lasting eight days.

Chanukah Gelt   Money given as a gift at Chanukah time.

Chol HaMoed   The intervening days between the first and last days of Passover or Succoth, considered half-holidays.

Dreidel   Four-sided top played with on Chanukah.

Esther   The heroic queen in the Book of Esther. She saved her people from destruction.

Ethrog   Citrus fruit, resembling a large lemon, used on Succoth.

Grogger   Noise maker used on Purim.

Hagadah   Book read at the Seder on Passover evening.

Haman   The villain in the Book of Esther who wanted to destroy the Jews.

Haman Tasch   Three-cornered cakes, filled with poppy-seeds or prunes, eaten on Purim.

Hora   Israeli group dance.

Kiddush   Prayer or blessing said over wine before the meal on Sabbaths and holidays.

Lag B'Omer   Thirty-third day, counting from the second day of Passover.

L'Shanah Tovah   A New Year greeting meaning, "May you have a good year!"

Lulav   A palm branch combined with willow and myrtle leaves, used on the Succoth holiday.

Matzoh   Unleavened bread eaten during Passover.

Megillah   Scroll, usually refers to the Book of Esther read on Purim.

Menorah   Frequently refers to the special candle-holder for Chanukah, with its eight branches.

Mordecai   Queen Esther's cousin in the Purim story.

Oneg Shabbat   Sabbath joy, a happy gathering or party on the Sabbath.

GLOSSARY

Passover   Holiday commemorating the liberation of the Israelites from slavery in Egypt.

Pesach   Hebrew name for Passover.

Purim   Feast of Lots told about in the Book of Esther.

Rosh Chodesh   The New Moon, tht beginning of the Hebrew month.

Rosh Hashanah   Hebrew New Year.

Seder   Service celebrated at home on the first two nights of Passover.

Shabbat   Sabbath, Saturday.

Shabbat Shalom   A Sabbath greeting meaning, "May you have a peaceful Sabbath!"

Shalach Manoth   Sending gifts, usually food, on Purim.

Shavuoth   Feast of Weeks, comes seven weeks after the second day of Passover.

Shofar   Ram's horn.

Simchat Torah   Holiday of rejoicing of the Torah.

Succah   Booth, hut.

Succoth   The Feast of Booths or Tabernacles, lasts eight days.

Torah   Teaching, Law, the Five Books of Moses.

Tu B'Shvat   The fifteenth day of the Hebrew month of Shvat.

WEST END SYNAGOGUE
LIBRARY